Prophet
or Madman

Prophet
or Madman

A bridge between worlds

Bruce Adams

Prophet or Madman / Bruce Adams – 1st Edition.

Contains Glossary and Index

Library of Congress Control Number: 2005905140

ISBN: 0-9764840-6-4

Trinus Publishing

Trinus Publishing
21286 Hubbard Avenue
Port Charlotte, FL 33952

Acknowledgements

I wish to thank everyone who has touched my life and shared the many gifts this world has to offer.

Mostly, however, I wish to thank God for the experience of witnessing first-hand what it means to Love without conditions. I will never look at this world again through the "veil of ignorance" that I previously knew. My hope is that the message you entrusted to me has been conveyed here in a way that others can understand; with your help, may they gain the wisdom that has been lost to so many.

Wisdom speaks of its own rewards.

Happy is the man who listens to me, watching daily at my gates, waiting beside my doors. For he who finds me finds life and obtains favor from the LORD; but he who misses me injures himself; all who hate me love death.

Prov 8:34-36

Contents

Introduction

My name is Bruce Adams. I am neither a theologian, a Bible scholar, a pastor, nor a teacher. I was a businessman for some 25 years before I received the revelations from God that are included in this book. Before we start, I would like to give you some background on how this book came to be, and what it has meant to me.

I was born into an average middle-class family in Massachusetts in 1953. My parents raised me and my two brothers in the Roman Catholic Church. This was not because they had explored other belief systems and were convinced that they had found absolute truth, but rather because their parents, as well as their grandparents before them, had been raised in this tradition. Like many others who follow the teachings of the Church, my parents were quasi-Christians who seldom attended Mass but always made sure to observe the special holy days such as Christmas and Easter.

I have always been questioning and seeking answers. As a child, I often heard those pat answers so many people throw out when they really don't understand: "God has a plan for our life," and "Everything happens for a reason." Despite the fact that my mother's divorce and remarriage got her excommunicated from the Church, she sent both my brother and me to Catechism School to learn how to be good Christians. I did my best to accept what I was told, although my personal experiences were continually prompting me to turn inward and search for a higher Truth.

Flash forward to 1996. I had just sold a vending company as well as a dry cleaner's shop in Fort Myers, Florida. I had owned and operated these businesses in order to earn the financial capital needed to launch a moneymaking machine. I didn't need to be the richest man in the world—just wealthy enough to enable me to do anything I wanted at any time! I did not want to worry about working again for the rest of my life, and I believed that I had the means to realize this dream immediately.

My plan was to start a national company to sell a revolutionary new product, an over-the-counter herbal-based formula designed to speed up the rate at which the body metabolized alcohol. This product had the potential to save lives by sobering up drunken people much more quickly, possibly preventing accidents, and it also could have had the effect of lessening or eliminating hangovers.

I had worked on developing this project full-time for about a year, and had invested a great deal of money in test marketing and planning. Everything was falling into place; the projections indicated that, at the current sales rate in test locations, my new venture would soon be netting millions of dollars per month. Needless to say, I was very pleased with these numbers and eager to get started. That time appeared to be quickly approaching. I had distribution set up across the country, just waiting for the product. I had a supplier ready to handle production. I had an internal auditing system in place to track everything. I felt comfortable that everything was ready—and then I had the surprise of my life.

There is an expression my mother used quite frequently when I was a kid: "Man proposes and God disposes." I was about to find out first-hand that, indeed, there is an interaction between God and this world.

The Saturday after picking up the newly designed formula, I took my 9-year-old son Michael and one of his friends ice-skating. As a child, I used to love skating, so I joined in, letting all my cares go and living "in the moment." There I was, gliding along, listening to the music...when all of a sudden, *something happened*. The music, as well as the sound of the people, seemed to fall silent, just as if I had become temporarily deaf. The next thing I heard was a voice.

This voice was unlike anything that I had ever heard in the past. It seemed to be not limited to my mind, but dimensional. By this, I mean that it was both internal and audible at the same time. I did not know how to take what was happening to me, especially when I saw that I was being given specific instructions to change the direction of my life. I was being told to forego the project that was going to provide me with millions of dollars and early luxury retirement, because there was something else I had to do. I was being instructed to start an herbal company and sell herbal supplements.

The author in 1996

Hearing this voice was surely the strangest thing I had ever experienced. It did not take long for things to get even more unbelievable. I did not know what was happening to me. I recall thinking: Is this Candid Camera? Not fully accepting the reality of it all, I was not sure what to do, and at the same time I felt I had no choice but to play along.

To say I was dumbfounded would be a ridiculous understatement. This was by far the most incredible experience I had ever had…and yet, somehow, I never wanted the moment to end. I continued to ask questions. As if I were speaking to a friend, I asked, "So what should I call this company?" The answer I received was *aha*. What does that mean, I asked. The answer was immediate and clear: "*A Healthy Alternative.*"

This was so far beyond anything I had ever experienced that I decided to keep the whole thing to myself. I remember thinking, "I can't even tell my wife about this, because she would immediately believe that I've lost my mind!"

Late that very night, around two in the morning, I finally went to bed and proceeded to pray as I always did. As I recounted the inexplicable events of the afternoon, I asked God to confirm what I believed I had heard. I remember feeling very confused; I did not want to accept what I was told to do with my life. While on the one hand, I was overjoyed with the prospect of God speaking to me, it was too much to just drop everything and follow blindly.

Part of me was really hoping that, somehow, what had happened was not real. "Maybe I can forget it and get back to my plans," I told myself. On the other hand I asked myself, "What if the experience *was* real: could I refuse to listen to God's instructions?" I was in such a struggle over what to do that I decided I could not handle this on my own. I also felt I could not ask anyone for help, for fear that they would think me crazy. With nowhere else to go, I decided to ask God.

There I was at 2:00 a.m., in bed beside my sleeping wife. I began with a prayer, and then proceeded to ask the question in my mind without speaking a word out loud. "Was what I heard today real?" Immediately my wife pronounced the word, "Yes." My first reaction was again in the form of a question. This time, however, the question was directed more to me. I was talking to myself and questioning whether I had really heard what I heard. Or did I imagine it? Could I have somehow imagined everything? I could not help doubting, and the question kept repeating itself over and over: What is happening? Is this real?

My mind continued racing, and nothing seemed to fit into the old box I previously saw as my world. Was my wife awake? Had she somehow heard me speaking? I thought again how my words to God were not audible, but spoken in silence within my mind. I had to find out for myself—was my wife asleep? I turned to her and quietly asked in a voice no louder than a whisper: "Are you awake?" There was no response; it seemed she was fast asleep. This meant she could not have heard me ask the question. So how did she respond to it?

Although I could not deny what had happened, there still there was a part of me that refused to accept things as they appeared to be. I did not want to let my dream die. After all, I had spent over a year preparing for my great moment, and now the payoff was upon me. In the hope that, somehow, I could forego the surrender of all my dreams and expectations for my life, I asked again: "Are you sure this is something I must do?" Instantly I was answered—the word "Yes" came forth from my wife once again, to erase any doubt as to the validity of what I was hearing.

It was at this point that I accepted that it was time for me to investigate a realm different from the one I had previously adopted as my world. It would be years before I completed the transition from seeing things strictly through physical eyes to perceiving them with my newly opening spiritual ones; nevertheless, I had taken the first step.

Although not sure about how to continue, I decided to devote a certain amount of time each day to developing a stronger connection to this inner world. The method I chose was through the practice of meditation. At first I spent only a few minutes a day sitting in silence, attempting to quiet the chatter that I had grown to accept as normal. Little by little, I extended the time spent consciously shifting my attention inward. At first, the idea of sitting in quiet reflection left me feeling that there was something missing. Where was God? How come nothing was happening? I felt I was doing my part and yet, after a few weeks, I began to think I was wasting my time. After all, only a short time earlier, I had heard God speak to me!

Still I persevered, night after night, week after week. At last, one night, something different began to happen. I started off in the way I had grown accustomed to when meditating. I put on some music and sat in a chair, all the while focusing on opening myself beyond this world. I cleared my mind of any thoughts and asked to see things as God sees them. One moment I felt peaceful; in the next, I experienced a sensation that seemed very different indeed. I was becoming aware of my body in a way that felt different. It seemed as though I and my body were not one. While I understood that my body belonged to me, I felt as though it were a heavy coat restricting me, locking me inside somehow. Part of me knew that I could shed the coat and be free, but something stopped me. What was I afraid of, I asked myself? That night, the closest I came to experiencing the conscious release of my body was to feel a trembling throughout, as though at any moment I would break free.

About three weeks later the same sensation came over me— and this time I decided to go along with it. This time, after the trembling started, I moved my focus from outside to inside. I saw the body more clearly than at any other time in my life. In that moment, I knew that I could allow my brain to tell me that the feeling of paralysis I was having was not real. I decided to explore what was to come. The next thing I remember was that (somehow) I was out of my body, standing on the other side of the room, observing myself as I sat in a chair. This experience led me to want to explore this world in even greater depth. It was a world that had previously existed outside of my level of Awareness.

I continued my regimen of daily meditation. Sometimes I would meditate for hours. My perception of life drastically changed, and was replaced with something far different. Life, it seemed, was taking on new meaning. Faith that there was something more was replaced with direct experience.

I remember considering whether I would write the book that Spirit had instructed me to write about spirituality. My human, intellectual mind went into overdrive. I started off by telling myself that I had no formal training when it came to writing. Also, I had to deal with perhaps a greater obstacle: I believed that if I wrote a book that had a negative influence on others, I would be responsible for the results. Not wanting to chance such a thing, I decided to postpone the writing until I had more clarity. I vowed to myself that I would not go forward until all doubts had been removed.

Gradually, my perceptions started to present new pictures. With my vision shifting from the limited world as my reality to seeing life as an infinite experience, my personal relationships became a distraction to my writing. It was necessary to rent an apartment where I could find the solitude required in order to focus. Monday through Friday, I lived apart from my family and would meditate day and night. After a few months of this kind of concentration, I had an experience that took away any remaining doubts as to whether I should write the book or not.

That day I got up in the morning and set my mind on the ultimate objectives. I was becoming more accustomed to my new vision, and things like the Bible were starting to become clearer. My attachment to the circumstances of everyday life was becoming more burdensome. Old thought patterns constantly attempted to enter my mind, and often these thoughts would make me feel lonely, as though I were living in an alien world. At these times, I felt like giving up the whole idea and returning home to what was familiar.

I often found it helpful to take a break and go for a walk. There, I would connect with nature. I would walk around the neighbourhood and watch people coming and going. Cars, trucks, bikes would go by and I would imagine all the different experiences the people were having. I remember asking myself: How many (if any) of these people really understand why they are in this world? It seemed to me that most people were so caught up in their lives, running here and running there, that they were only partially awake.

I would ask myself over and over, why is this world so blind? How is it that so many can be so confused over the big picture? What is it that I am to share? The answer came to me one night, around 2:30 in the morning. I had gone to bed about midnight, after spending much of the evening meditating and writing. There was nothing in particular on my mind when I retired.

Throughout most of my life, I very rarely remembered my dreams upon awakening; dreams had not had too much impact on me. This night was not like most nights. I was sleeping and unaware of anything that was going on in my dream state, when I experienced something that made the voice I heard earlier seem trivial in comparison.

The best I can describe it is to say that I felt wide awake, yet I knew that my body was resting. I was both in the body and outside it. I could think, but there was no need to. I saw myself, for the lack of a better word, as a *formless Consciousness*. Where was I? There was nothing familiar about this place, because it had no form, and at the same time there was the sensation of comfort. It was like the feeling of comfort you have in the safety of your own home.

Formlessness still carries a meaning to many, because the mind needs to associate every experience with something familiar from the past. In the moment of this experience, I had no such struggle. It was only when I attempted to share this experience that I faced this problem. Did you ever hear the expression, "The words get in the way"? If you wish to understand more of anything, the first thing you must do is open yourself to seeing more than what you have accepted. All of Creation—in all of its forms—has its origin in a formless consciousness.

In retrospect, my mind seemed to be part of a consciousness where there was no Separation, and yet somehow I was still Me. With this experience, I can say that I truly know first-hand what was meant by the statement in the Bible, "We live, move and have our being (in God)." In that moment, I became aware of the whole of Creation as one presence. Upon coming back into my thinking mind,

I recall being told to write about what I had experienced. I jumped out of bed and got my pad and pen. I started to write. The Matrix of Creation was all that I could put onto the pad in that moment. Somehow mere words could never convey what I had just witnessed.

As I continued my writing and looked at the Bible, the Koran, the Bhagavad-Gita, and anything else that spoke of God, I saw that they all proclaimed their proximity to Truth. I cannot say that there is one scripture that contains the perfect Truth that you should follow. What I can tell you is that, if you ask in earnest, you will be led to a higher level of understanding. *Prophet or Madman* was written in, and contains, a very high or elevated Consciousness; it requires you to open to Unconditional Love in order to realize its full impact.

An Important Note to the Reader

Much of what follows may at times seem to be contradictory. Some of it may coincide with traditional interpretations, while other material might prove difficult to understand. This is because, unlike other books, this work is not the result of extensive research and study. It is the product of a direct revelation from God.

God has told me that my purpose in this world is to explain and clarify the message of Christ. Hence this book. The words that follow are not my words or my interpretations, but rather the words and interpretations of *he who sent me*. Unlike many prophets of the past you might be familiar with, men who received their divine calling via intermediaries such as angels, visions, etc., I am the beneficiary of communication with the Creator himself. What I know is what he told me. Direct.

Although I recognize that the Father and I are one, I am not the Father (Creator) but his messenger. I am going to share with you not only the real meaning behind scripture, but also an overview of the mechanics of Creation. This book will not only give you the roadmap to salvation—it will provide you with an insight into God's consciousness.

> *Then he opened their minds to understand the scriptures...*
>
> Luke 24:45

Understanding scripture can be difficult. Not only must you often look at things from an entirely different perspective, but you must also reconsider the meanings of certain words. Old or entrenched meanings and interpretations can frequently get in the way of understanding.

Many of the words used in this book can only be understood from a new perspective. A word "seen" through Spiritual eyes has a different meaning from one "seen" through human eyes. To help the reader, I have used capital letters (upper case) to denote Spiritual concepts, and lower case for words describing human or worldly ones. For example, the word "Creator," when referring to God, uses the capital "C"; when referring to Man as a creator, it uses a lower case "c." Similarly, the word "god" might be used, as opposed to "God"—there are many gods, but there is only one God or Creator force.

To truly grasp what is in this book, you will have to give a new meaning to everything that you think you already know.

Part One: Christ and Truth

Who was Jesus, and what did he teach? Was he the savior prophesied in the Old Testament?

In this Part, we are going to examine and answer these questions. We are also going to see how and why so many people have misunderstood Jesus and missed the Truth.

To add some clarity, it is a good idea to begin by understanding that Christ was not Jesus' last name, but rather his title. Christ is the English version of the Greek *Khristos*, which means "the Anointed" or "the Messiah."

The Messiah prophesied in the Old Testament was misunderstood 2000 years ago, and continues to be misunderstood today. What is the source of this confusion? As in many other things, the source can best be found at the beginning—and this is the most logical place to begin our search. However, before we start, let us talk about the Bible in general.

1. Interpreting the Bible

Many people will pick up a book and read the ending before the beginning, because they have a natural curiosity about the outcome. It seems that as long as Man is thinking and engaging the human mind (brain), this form of linear thinking will continue. It has always been the norm. Unfortunately, this will not help you with the Bible.

The Bible is a combination of many stories. It consists of two parts. The first part (the Old Testament or Hebrew Bible) lays the foundation for Creation and Man's adventure from Oneness to Separation from God. It then proceeds to demonstrate that state of Separation in narrative form. Since there is in truth no Separation possible between God and Man (something we shall be discussing at length in the course of this book), the Old Testament also includes many stories about those who displayed the ability to transcend the limits of the Human experience. These persons were called Prophets by some and crazy by others.

> **Separation**
> A perceived experience, based on the belief that something can exist outside of All That Is (God).

Among those who had the ability to see beyond the illusion of the world of Man, and connect with a higher consciousness, was Moses. When he was at a true level of Awareness, he was instructed to present the Law or Torah, for men to live by. As Einstein teaches us, everything is relative—and so it was with the Law. Because our minds had no past experience with which to weigh or judge each moment, it was vital to set up laws to act as guidelines. The purpose of these rules was to govern men's behavior, and to teach people how to co-exist in a world of perceived Separation. In other words, to teach them how to become good and moral human beings in an evolutionary experience geared toward self-discovery—The Death Experience.

The second part of the Bible, also known as the New Testament, contains a lot of the same information. Nevertheless, a shift does take place. This shift involves moving beyond the idea of merely becoming a good human, to the point of actually accepting the Consciousness of the Oneness again (i.e., Rebirthing). Many people have heard that they must be "born again" in order to establish for themselves a place in Heaven; in fact, this is the primary message of the New Testament. You could say that the New Testament is a progression or fulfillment of the Old Testament, and as such, it requires you to expand your vision. This shift will move you from darkness (Death) to light (Life).

To get the full impact of what you are about to read, I would ask you again to open your mind and let go of all previously-held notions of what you may hear. Many terms will not seem clear, or if familiar, they might carry meanings different from those you are used to. If something does not show itself clearly, it may be necessary to re-read that section while opening to your Inner Sight. It is only your Inner Sight (Higher Self) that can recognize Truth.

Although I have included many references to the Christian Bible, I do not feel that is the *only* source of Truth. Why do I say this? **Truth** belongs to God and is universal, beyond Man's perceptions. The Bible is one source of Truth, although it often is a source of misconceptions and misinterpretations. Once you accept a misinterpretation as Truth, it is extremely difficult to change your mind back to Reality. If

> **Truth**
> That which is beyond perception.

you asked a thousand people (or a thousand pastors) to interpret the Bible for you, you might get a thousand different interpretations. This makes it easy for manipulation to take place on a large scale. An example of this occurred in Nazi Germany, where so many people accepted atrocities because they believed falsely, and let a demented leader determine what was true for them.

However, let us get back to the story in the Bible. Please note that it is just that: a story. There are times when you must discern what is to be taken literally and what is to be taken as a metaphor. The Book of Genesis contains many metaphors, and will often require you to go beyond your human mind. If you wish to understand fully, it is very important that you spend time experiencing the meaning of the words, or you will remain in the same confused state you have previously embraced as your version of reality.

For those who wish to research further on their own, you will find that there are various translations of the Bible. While most are similar, there are some that may use more or less modern language, some that aim at an exact, word-for-word translation, some that eschew certain terms, etc. I have chosen the Revised Standard Version, not because it is the easiest to understand, but because it steers a middle ground between many of these competing translation methodologies.

2. In the Beginning...

> *In the beginning God created the heavens and the earth. The earth was without form and void, and darkness was upon the face of the deep; and the Spirit of God was moving over the face of the waters. And God said, "Let there be light"; and there was light.*
>
> Gen 1:1-3

After reading Genesis for myself, I realized how distorted my previous understanding was. In fact, the text spoke of many things that were not only different from, but often in direct contradiction to, my past beliefs. Through my experience, I realized that if you are interested in an in-depth study of the Bible, you must find the time to be with it on your own.

Because the Bible contains so much information and covers so many levels of awareness, I felt it would be best if I address only the points that have fostered the greatest confusion.

One such point is the idea that God is a man. If you remember that **God** is the summation of all that is, you must recognize that it is impossible for God to be limited to Form of any kind.

> **God**
> That Which Is.
> The summation
> of everything.

> *So God created man in his own image, in the image of God he created him; male and female he created them.*
>
> Gen 1:27

To all who hold to the notion that God is a man, all I can say is: you may want to reconsider! To all those women who have embraced the idea of the "Goddess" as being the form of God, I would offer the same advice. The truth is that God may possess the energy of both male and female, but God is formless and without gender in Ultimate Reality.

> *Male and female he created them, and he blessed*
> *them and named them Man when they were*
> *created.*
>
> Gen 5:2

Here it is reiterated that it takes both forms of energy to make the whole, and neither is complete without the other. I do not mean to imply that it is necessary to be in a relationship with the opposite sex in order to be complete; I am saying that, at the level of energy beyond physical matter, there is a merging of the sexes. They become one.

The World beyond Time and Space

In Genesis 2:4, you will find your first hint of the concept of past, present, and future existing as one.

> *These are the generations of the heavens and the*
> *earth when they were created. In the day that the*
> *LORD God made the earth and the heavens...*
>
> Gen 2:4

Notice that the generations of heavens (that is, the ones to come) were created in the day that God made the earth and the heavens. This is to help you begin to understand that, in Ultimate Reality, *Time* as Man understands it does not exist. I will talk about this in greater detail in Part Two, but for now it is enough to say that what *seems* Real and what *is* Real are two very different things.

> *...then the LORD God formed man of dust from the*
> *ground, and breathed into his nostrils the breath of*
> *life; and man became a living being.*
>
> Gen 2:7

Acceptance of the fact that there is a real distinction between the body and the soul is a prerequisite to correct understanding of this passage; otherwise, you run the risk of a faulty interpretation based on distorted perception. First, God formed the body. Then he introduced the soul to the body. Later in the Bible you will find that

> *No one has ascended into heaven but he who descended from heaven...*
>
> Jn 3:13

When you put both these statements together, a picture is formed that starts to make sense. The breath of life is referring to the soul that already exists in Heaven (another dimension), and it is placed in the body for a different type of experience.

Getting back to the story: let's pick it up from the Garden of Eden, at the portrayal of the Fall from Grace. The story began by setting the stage for Man to experience himself as one with God, as well as with the rest of Creation. It was at this point, where Love (or Oneness) was the only thing that existed, that both Adam and Eve lived in Paradise with no fear. Fear, shame, guilt, worry, sorrow, regret, and grief were all alien to their minds; there was no opposition to Love. Without such an opposite, there was no Duality, and no need to judge. However, all that changed in one moment. If you compare Gen 2:25, 3:7, and 3:10, you will see that there was a major change in the state of consciousness of these human beings, and as we read further, what transpired becomes even clearer.

> *And the man and his wife were both naked, and were not ashamed.*
>
> Gen 2:25

> *Then the eyes of both were opened, and they knew that they were naked; and they sewed fig leaves together and made themselves aprons.*
>
> Gen 3:7

What eyes do you suppose this passage is referring to?

And he said, "I heard the sound of thee in the garden, and I was afraid, because I was naked; and I hid myself."

Gen 3:10

If God created Adam and Eve naked, why was Adam so afraid of being naked all of a sudden? The answers to these questions can be found in the warning God had given about not eating of the Tree of Knowledge, the one standing beside the Tree of Life in the middle of the garden. Do you remember this warning?

But of the tree of the knowledge of good and evil you shall not eat, for in the day that you eat of it you shall die.

Gen 2:17

According to the story, they did indeed eat of the Tree of Knowledge of Good and Evil, defying the Lord's warning—and, unless you choose to believe that God lied to them, *they died that very day*.

We have now encountered a term that has created some of the greatest fear and confusion known to Man.

The word *Death* conjures up tremendous fear. Why? Because most people can only relate to their physical bodies. We have just read that God breathed the breath of life into the body and the body became a living soul. What people have forgotten is that their souls are eternal, and as such, have existed prior to transference into the body.

So what then is meant by the death mentioned in Genesis? I hope that you are starting to understand that the death alluded to is not physical, but refers to one's vision or consciousness relative to the whole of Creation.

If you look up "death" in the dictionary, you will find that it is usually defined as a departure, a passing, or a destruction of something. In this particular case, all of these are indeed happening—but not in physical terms. The death is one of *Consciousness*. Such a loss of awareness leaves a feeling of Separation/Fear that is not based upon Truth, but rather upon a false perception of what is True.

If you continue to open yourself and accept that God is indeed omnipresent, you will discover that any perception of separation from God is in fact illusory, existing only within the confines of your mind.

For those who have understood this, and yet still believe in the permanence of death, there is this verse from much later in the Bible:

> *For as by a man came death, by a man has come*
> *also the resurrection of the dead.*
>
>   1 Cor 15:21

Why do you suppose this does not say, "Death came from God"? Moreover, how do you resurrect from something, if that something is final?

As with everything you can (and will) experience, death is based on a *belief*. As long as you hold to the idea of something, you are setting the energy in motion to bring about the experience associated with that belief. Anything you experience in time is triggered by a thought; for that reason, judgment based on perceptions will not always be true. All perceptions are relative; they can and do change.

> *Put your hand on a hot stove for a minute, and it*
> *seems like an hour. Sit with a pretty girl for an*
> *hour, and it is like a minute. THAT'S relativity.*
>
>   Albert Einstein

Getting back to the Garden of Eden: here is a metaphor for the essential choice we all face in every moment. On one hand, we have the Tree of Life (Oneness/Life); on the other hand, the Tree of Knowledge of Good and Evil (Separation/Death). Another way to look at this is to say that we are always offered this choice: either to live in Oneness (Love), or to experience Separation (Fear/Death). One look at this world will suffice to show very clearly there are few people who recognize the fundamental truth that every single person is an expression of God, and worthy of *Unconditional Love*.

We have already covered a lot of ground, beginning with the story of Creation itself. Next came Man, and then the choice of Love or Fear as an experience. (By the way: isn't it interesting that, according to the story, Adam and Eve chose the Tree of Judgment—where **Duality** is at the center?)

> **Duality**
> A system based on opposites: positive and negative, good and bad, awake and asleep, Life and Death, etc.

We then got to see first-hand the introduction of Cause and Effect, explaining how it could be said that "by a man came death." In Reality, the term *death* is synonymous with the experience of Separation—which in turn is triggered by choice. So in fact, Adam and Eve are not responsible for your living outside of Paradise. In Reality, what you experience results from the choices *you* have made.

Yes, you read that correctly. I am saying that it is up to you, and you alone, to experience something that is not real, based in illusion and fear, or to experience Reality in Love.

In every moment you are either consciously connected, focused on the whole of Creation as a single presence, or you are maintaining false beliefs that narrow your vision. This is the sum difference between life and death. In life, you come from the One, are still One, and will always be One with the wholeness that is God.

In the illusion of death, you experience the fear of Separation, and are condemned to judge everything relative to a perceived past.

The Moment of Choice in the Garden of Eden

Tree of Life
Aware of
God
and
the rest of
Creation

or

**Tree of Knowledge
of Good and Evil**
*The Death
Experience;
perceived
separation from* **God**

Paradise

The world of Man

*Arrows represent
Man's path from
Death back
to Life*

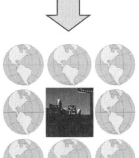

The way to Heaven
Love-Light-Awake

Our physical world
Fear-Darkness-Asleep

The Journey Home

Where is home, and how do you get there? Ask anyone where he or she is from, and you will hear some reference to a place or location on this Earth. It seems that very few are consciously aware enough to remember their real home.

Looking back to where we left off in Genesis, you might see why there is such confusion. According to the story, Adam and Eve were at home in Eden without a care in the world, and the next moment they found themselves in such fear that Adam hid when he heard God's voice. It seems that their new home had changed radically for the worse. Love was replaced by Fear, and guilt and shame became the predominant energies. The Lord, not wanting this fallen state (living in Ego) to become a permanent condition, drove them out of the garden and placed an angel with a flaming sword to keep them from the Tree of Life.

Some might ask, Why did God keep them from eating from the Tree of Life? By driving them out of the garden, he was protecting them from transforming their temporary state of Separation into a permanent condition. He knew that they had to go through a purification process before they were ready to once again move into an eternal experience. Because they were living in a world of Illusion and Fear, they had to be purged of all false beliefs.

As you read the story of the Bible, you will find that it is a story that contains many levels of Awareness within the dream state of Man. These levels lead up to a point of readiness and a re-birthing back to Love (Oneness).

The Story of Cain and Abel

Within the system symbolized by the Tree of Knowledge of Good and Evil, you will find opposites to everything. This system of polarities is the basis for all experiences perceived as life in the three-dimensional world we inhabit. To understand this system it is helpful to remember that polarities depict diametric opposition, and as such have a tendency to cancel each other out. By this I mean that positive will balance negative, and negative will balance positive, until a state of neutral is reached. This is what has been called perfect harmony: a state where there is no bad and there is no good. Only in this state is it possible to experience the vibration of Unconditional Love.

The story of Cain and Abel is a good example of the complexities of such a system. Here you find a love/hate relationship that comprises the full spectrum of emotion. The story also shows which energy is the most prominent in the human condition. After the shift (eating of the Tree of Knowledge of Good and Evil) took place, Man was no longer consciously aware of perfect harmony/Unconditional Love. In fact, he was experiencing its exact opposite, Fear (*f*alse *e*vidence *a*ppearing to be *r*eal). Once Fear had become the predominate energy, Man came to believe that he had to earn God's love through sacrifice. It would seem that a belief had been established, that what was once freely given in Oneness now had to be earned in Separation. Such are the rules that accompany the fear-based thought system of Man.

> *Now Adam knew Eve his wife, and she conceived*
> *and bore Cain, saying, "I have gotten a man with*
> *the help of the LORD."*
>
> Gen 4:1

Notice that, after they had undergone the Death Experience that was promised by God, Eve conceived and Cain was born. How would this be possible if they were both dead? This will become clearer later as you read of the *second death* spoken of in the New Testament. If things are to make sense later, then you must realize that the Death referred to here is a spiritual one. When God promised Adam and Eve that they would immediately die, he was not referring to the passing away of the physical body, but to conscious awareness of the rest of Creation.

> *And again, she bore his brother Abel. Now Abel*
> *was a keeper of sheep, and Cain a tiller of the*

ground. In the course of time Cain brought to the
LORD an offering of the fruit of the ground, and
Abel brought of the firstlings of his flock and of
their fat portions. And the LORD had regard for
Abel and his offering, but for Cain and his offering
he had no regard. So Cain was very angry, and his
countenance fell.

Gen 4:2-5

What a great example of the power of our Judgment, and the
effect it has on our experience! As Cain followed his belief that his
brother had outdone him, he became extremely angry. It seems that
it did not take long for jealousy to find its way into the human mind.

The LORD said to Cain, "Why are you angry, and
why has your countenance fallen? If you do well,
will you not be accepted? And if you do not do well,
sin is couching at the door; its desire is for you, but
you must master it."

Gen 4:6-7

The Lord attempts to correct Cain's confused mind, and tells
him it is enough to do his best; it is not a competition between him
and his brother.

Cain said to Abel his brother, "Let us go out to the
field." And when they were in the field, Cain rose
up against his brother Abel, and killed him.

Gen 4:8

Not accepting that God looked upon him with the same
degree of love, Cain felt that the best solution was to eliminate the
competition by killing his brother.

Then the LORD said to Cain, "Where is Abel your
brother?" He said, "I do not know; am I my
brother's keeper?" And the LORD said, "What have
you done? The voice of your brother's blood is
crying to me from the ground. And now you are

cursed from the ground, which has opened its mouth to receive your brother's blood from your hand. When you till the ground, it shall no longer yield to you its strength; you shall be a fugitive and a wanderer on the earth." Cain said to the LORD, "My punishment is greater than I can bear. Behold, thou hast driven me this day away from the ground; and from thy face I shall be hidden; and I shall be a fugitive and a wanderer on the earth, and whoever finds me will slay me." Then the LORD said to him, "Not so! If any one slays Cain, vengeance shall be taken on him sevenfold." And the LORD put a mark on Cain, lest any who came upon him should kill him. Then Cain went away from the presence of the LORD, and dwelt in the land of Nod, east of Eden. Cain knew his wife, and she conceived and bore Enoch; and he built a city, and called the name of the city after the name of his son, Enoch.

Gen 4:9-16

For those who do not yet understand that these stories are not to be taken literally, ask yourself the following: If Cain and Abel along with their parents Adam and Eve were the only people on Earth, whom was Cain referring to when he feared for his life? And where did Cain's wife come from?

The story of Cain and Abel depicts how far Man had fallen from Love, and shows how the first murder was rationalized in the mind. Instead of Love and Oneness, Fear and Separation had become the dominating influences. We are witness to the burden of dealing with the most negative energy, the extreme point on the Ego's journey.

If you were to continue to read Genesis, you would find that the wickedness of Man continued in generation after generation, leading up to the time of the Great Flood (the Cleansing).

The LORD saw that the wickedness of man was great in the earth, and that every imagination of the thoughts of his heart was only evil continually. And the LORD was sorry that he had made man on the earth, and it grieved him to his heart. So the LORD said, "I will blot out man whom I have created from the face of the ground, man and beast and creeping things and birds of the air, for I am sorry that I have made them."

Gen 6:5-7

According to the story about the Great Flood, God cleansed the earth of the evil that had developed; then he acknowledged that this evil is innate to the heart of Man. In other words, evil is the default for the human mind. In story after story in the Old Testament, you will find that Man is constantly at odds with his Spiritual essence (Love). Repeatedly, the consequences of choosing Evil/Ego over Good/Spirit are demonstrated. The Ego is king in the world of Man, and for that reason, the Law had to be introduced. The Law (Torah) I am referring to was made up of many laws, and if you read all the so-called Books of Moses (the Pentateuch, the first five books in the Old Testament), you will become more familiar with it.

"Evil is the default for the human mind."

Rather than recount every story contained in the Old Testament, I will feel it would be more helpful to summarize it as one story—the way it was originally meant to be understood. Starting at the beginning, it introduces the formation of the three-dimensional World (the physical universe. Next, Man is introduced as a body to house the Soul; this is done in order to allow the Soul to experience itself in the form of matter. The lower vibration of the body proves to be too much for the Soul, and the connectedness or link to All That Is becomes veiled; it is replaced by a world of Illusion based on perception. No longer is Man governed by Love (Oneness). Fear becomes the influence or initiator of each experience.

God, seeing that Man has chosen to live in the world of Illusion and Separation, introduced laws necessary to govern the world. Because God is all-loving, the Creator of all things (including Man), these laws were not based on reward and punishment governed by Judgment, but rather on Love, focused on Cause and Effect. The purpose of these laws was and is to present in each moment an opportunity for Man to remember his real identity: a child of the one Creator, all that was and All That Is.

Until one returns to Love and Oneness, the best that one can hope for is to become a good Ego. This is the theme of the Old Testament. It teaches people to follow the letter of the Law and become the best Ego they can become. It is not until the New Testament that the idea is introduced that becoming a good Ego is merely a step along the path toward full Awareness (re-birthing). Until this re-birthing occurs, you will continue to experience your journey trapped within the confines of Hell.

3. The Christel

What was Jesus' Message to the World?
How did He Differ from Others before Him?

In order to correctly answer these questions, it will be helpful to look at the overall message of the New Testament. As the name indicates, the New Testament was not just a continuation of the past but also an introduction to something new and different.

In the beginning of the Bible, we read that Man was created by God, was in direct communication with him, and was under Grace. The Fall from Grace came from Man's choosing to ignore God's command not to judge his world, in spite of the warning that they would die that very day. Once they began to see things with human instead of divine eyes, they were forced to leave Paradise. When Man chooses to see or interpret things in this way, the experience that results is called Death. This Death, or Hell, can continue forever—but it is not necessarily eternal.

> *Consider and answer me, O LORD my God; lighten*
> *my eyes, lest I sleep the sleep of death...*
>
> Ps 13:3

Since the beginning of time, most of us have not understood that there is a resurrection from the Death Experience, a re-birthing of Consciousness if you will. This re-birthing is an automatic result of choosing Love and God over personal desire for people or things in this world.

Choosing God is very difficult for us. Most people believe that it is impossible. That is why Jesus was sent from the Light (Love) into the world of Darkness (Fear). He came to demonstrate that, indeed, it *could* be done. If you take the time to understand and follow his example, it is certain that you will be transformed. You will experience rebirth, and come back to life.

Jesus spoke the same Truth and delivered the same message that you find at the core of most major religions. If I were to sum up the message of the Christ, I would say he delivered a perfect understanding of Love (God), first by explaining the words and then by becoming a living example. Christ demonstrated that it is possible to live while consciously connected to God.

> *So we know and believe the love God has for us.* God is love, *and he who abides in love abides in* God, *and God abides in him.*
>
> 1 Jn 4:16

At first glance, the message appears to be simple enough, so one might ask: Why is there still so much confusion? The answer is that Man is challenged when it comes to understanding. The words we use get in the way. For example, take the word *love*: in almost all cases, it conjures up a certain image in the human mind. In addition, if that image is based on personal relationships rooted in the world of **Form**, relationships that overshadow the big picture, one cannot help but have a distorted view.

Form
The appearance of something relative to the senses.

The Unconditional Love that Jesus taught was not personal, but universal. It was contrary to how Man previously understood it. Not everyone can understand it fully even now. It is only after you develop your spiritual eyes and accept higher Truth that Jesus' teaching can be fully realized. Realization of Truth is a prerequisite to salvation. It is not enough simply to believe that Jesus came to die for our sins and is our Lord and Savior.

> *Not every one who says to me, 'Lord, Lord,' shall enter the kingdom of heaven, but he who does the will of my Father who is in heaven.*
>
> Mt 7:21

Is it possible for Man to understand and do the will of the Father, as Jesus instructed? To answer that question, it becomes necessary to know what Jesus said was the will of the Father. His response was clear:

> *And he answered, "You shall love the Lord your God with all your heart, and with all your soul, and with all your strength, and with all your mind; and your neighbor as yourself."*
>
> Lk 10:27

To love God means to go beyond that which serves **Ego**, and to live only for that which serves God. This means that *all things in this world* must be viewed through the eyes of your Higher Self. Failing to do this will always result in producing a distorted view based on Ego (i.e., that which is most important to the personal self).

> **Ego**
> The Lower Self:
> that part of Soul
> that identifies
> with the physical
> personality self
> of this world.

> *And he began to teach them that the Son of man must suffer many things, and be rejected by the elders and the chief priests and the scribes, and be killed, and after three days rise again. And he said this plainly. And Peter took him, and began to rebuke him. But turning and seeing his disciples, he rebuked Peter, and said, "Get behind me, Satan! For you are not on the side of God, but of men." And he called to him the multitude with his disciples, and said to them, "If any man would come after me, let him deny himself and take up his cross and follow me. For whoever would save his life will lose it; and whoever loses his life for my sake and the gospel's will save it. For what does it profit a man, to gain the whole world and forfeit his life? For what can a man give in return for his life? For whoever is ashamed of me and of my words in this adulterous and sinful generation, of*

him will the Son of man also be ashamed, when he comes in the glory of his Father with the holy angels."

Mk 8:31-38

This is a good example of how Ego's idea of love and Unconditional Love differ. Peter, in his humanness, was speaking from his Ego mind when he rebuked Jesus. Peter was allowing his feelings of attachment to Jesus to cloud his Consciousness. Sometimes the feelings that we think are Love are in fact the exact opposite (Fear), originating in the Ego. Jesus made this clear when he referred to his apostle as Satan. Did Satan actually take over Peter's Consciousness? Or was it that Peter just moved into his Ego mind? (Try substituting the word "Ego" in place of "Satan" anywhere in the Bible for clarity.)

Do not delude yourself into thinking that you can have it both ways.

No one can serve two masters; for either he will hate the one and love the other, or he will be devoted to the one and despise the other. You cannot serve God and mammon.

Mt 6:24

If any of you lacks wisdom, let him ask God, who gives to all men generously and without reproaching, and it will be given him. But let him ask in faith, with no doubting, for he who doubts is like a wave of the sea that is driven and tossed by the wind. For that person must not suppose that a double-minded man, unstable in all his ways, will receive anything from the Lord.

Jas 1:5-8

Jesus Speaks of Unconditional Love

The Love that Jesus spoke of and the love that most people understand are worlds apart. In this world, the love that the majority of people feel is Ego-based and self-serving. In fact, it is conditional love that causes all the pain and suffering in this world. Love is not really in play—Fear is.

Knowing this, Jesus mentioned the need to raise the level of understanding of how we love. Everyone and everything must be seen in the same light. Not doing this adds more darkness (thickens the veil) and keeps true understanding from us. This is why he said that

> *...if any one comes to me and does not hate his own father and mother and wife and children and brothers and sisters, yes, and even his own life, he cannot be my disciple. Whoever does not bear his own cross and come after me, cannot be my disciple. For which of you, desiring to build a tower, does not first sit down and count the cost, whether he has enough to complete it? Otherwise, when he has laid a foundation, and is not able to finish, all who see it begin to mock him, saying, "This man began to build, and was not able to finish." Or what king, going to encounter another king in war, will not sit down first and take counsel whether he is able with ten thousand to meet him who comes against him with twenty thousand? And if not, while the other is yet a great way off, he sends an embassy and asks terms of peace. So therefore, whoever of you does not renounce all that he has cannot be my disciple.*
>
> Lk 14:26-33

Unlike human love, Unconditional Love cannot be limited or put into a box. Real love does not know jealousy, anger, hatred, or envy. Almost everyone in this world is experiencing conditional or personal love, loving with expectation and possessiveness.

"Unconditional Love cannot be limited or put into a box."

Most of us have been conditioned to believe in Separation since childhood. This is why the love that you feel for your family and the significant people in your life is usually different from what you feel for every other brother and sister in this world. It is the perceived Separation that we feel that creates conditional love. But if everyone and everything is God, how can there be any Separation? At some point, all things become One. The walls of Separation must come down.

The tribal belief system has served mankind in many ways along the path of the Soul's evolution. Many are locked into their primitive tribal beliefs. There are also those who are willing to go so far as to die for them. There are, however, many Souls in this world whose consciousness has elevated to the point where they are ready to move from conditional love to Unconditional Love.

When you observe war from the level of Unconditional Love, you can see how ridiculous it is to think that you are serving God by killing God. The only way men can justify war, or killing of any kind, is through their fear-based Ego mind, founded in the belief in Separation. This Ego mind belongs not to God but to the personal self. The good news is that God gave man the ability to overcome the human Ego mind and escape the confines of Hell. No one lacks this power—but one must choose to use it.

> *For God did not give us a spirit of timidity, but a spirit of power and love and self-control.*
> 2 Tim 1:7

As you read further, you will find that, not only do you have the power to influence your experiences, but you are also responsible for exercising control over your own mind. To begin to understand the choices available to you, it is helpful to remember that Love and Fear cannot coexist. If you are experiencing the one, you cannot have the other.

In his quest to teach that there is much more to life than Man had perceived, Jesus said:

> *You have heard that it was said, "You shall love your neighbor and hate your enemy." But I say to you, Love your enemies and pray for those who persecute you...*
>
> Mt 5:43-44

When you come to know yourself as Unconditional Love, you will then recognize your brother as yourself.

Jesus was the living example of Unconditional, divine Love. It did not matter to him how much money people had, where they lived, what color their skin was, or what they believed. Jesus recognized everyone as **Soul**, not as a personality.

Soul
That which was begotten of the Creator. The sum total of the I Am, the Ego, and the Higher Self.

> *And they sent their disciples to him, along with the Herodians, saying, "Teacher, we know that you are true, and teach the way of God truthfully, and care for no man; for you do not regard the position of men."*
>
> Mt 22:16

> *For if you love those who love you, what reward have you? Do not even the tax collectors do the same?*
>
> Mt 5:46

Jesus was making a point. To love those who love you is not difficult. It does not serve your highest good to limit your Love in any way.

*He who loves father or mother more than me is not
worthy of me; and he who loves son or daughter
more than me is not worthy of me.*

Mt 10:37

To love God means to see everyone through God's eyes. No
one is any more or less than the other. When you love your father,
mother, son or daughter more than you love any other person, you
are choosing conditional love. Do you love a cell in your foot more
than a cell in your leg? Until you can see the whole, you will be
limiting your capacity for love.

Ego-based love is easy to recognize. Bring someone or
something that you love into your Consciousness. Now ask yourself,
is the Love that you are expressing serving self or serving God?
Have you placed any conditions on this Love?

There are numerous parables in the Bible about love; they all
give the same message. All that it takes to see the truth is your
willingness to try. Jesus' message was an opportunity for souls to
see that they are already free. His example paved the way for Souls
to see past the illusions they were creating in this world. By his
teaching, there is no question that Soul is to choose the love of God
over love of Self.

Jesus Lived as a Human

*Therefore he had to be made like his brethren in
every respect, so that he might become a merciful
and faithful high priest in the service of God, to
make expiation for the sins of the people.*

Heb 2:17

In order to relate and know first-hand the pain and suffering Man
experiences in this world, Jesus lived a human experience. While
here, Jesus had to deal with the same wants, desires and temptations
that we all face. Although Jesus came to bring forth understanding,

he could have given in to his Ego and gotten lost in this world. He, too, was faced with the emotions and the challenge of dealing with the Ego (human) mind.

Prevalent is the false belief that Jesus was a man without sin. Throughout the New Testament, Jesus demonstrates qualities of both states of consciousness: that of Man (emotion) and that of Spirit (Unconditional Love).

In the following passage, Jesus is hungry as he approaches Jerusalem. How does he react to a fig tree without figs?

> *In the morning, as he was returning to the city, he was hungry. And seeing a fig tree by the wayside he went to it, and found nothing on it but leaves only. And he said to it, "May no fruit ever come from you again!" And the fig tree withered at once.*
>
> Mt 21:18-19

This was not an illustration of Love from one who was perfect and beyond Judgment. Clearly, Jesus was showing his disappointment that there was no fruit. Only the human mind could entertain, and then act upon, such an unloving act.

As a man, Jesus had moments of temptation. What made him different from other men, however, was that he came here to lay down his personal life (his Ego) and live a higher purpose.

> *For this reason the Father loves me, because I lay down my life, that I may take it again. No one takes it from me, but I lay it down of my own accord. I have power to lay it down, and I have power to take it again; this charge I have received from my Father.*
>
> Jn 10:17-18

By laying down his life, Jesus chose God over Ego. To appreciate the challenge Jesus faced, remember that at any moment Jesus could have surrendered to the temptation of the flesh (Ego) and lived for this world, not for God. What would you have done in the same circumstances?

Jesus Was No More God Than You Are!

Jesus fully acknowledged having an Ego, with all its frailties. Before full acceptance of the **Christ Consciousness**, Jesus recognized that he, too, was subject to moments of delusion (i.e., choosing the human experience over the Spiritual one); in those moments he was not perfect and was like any other man.

> **Christ Consciousness**
> The state of Awareness that is fully awakened to Perfect Love; being beyond all Judgment.

And Jesus said to him, "Why do you call me good? No one is good but God alone."
Lk 18:19

Jesus did not see himself as different or special. He reserved that distinction for God. He taught that all power was from the Father, not from him.

> *I can do nothing on my own authority; as I hear, I judge; and my judgment is just, because I seek not my own will but the will of him who sent me.*
> Jn 5:30

While it is true that Jesus was here to teach us to see beyond the personality self, he was not above having moments of being human. Examples of this, as I mentioned above, can be found in the Scriptures.

> *For because he himself has suffered and been tempted, he is able to help those who are tempted.*
> Heb 2:18

> *Then Jesus was led up by the Spirit into the wilderness to be tempted by the devil. And he*

fasted forty days and forty nights, and afterward he was hungry. And the tempter came and said to him, "If you are the Son of God, command these stones to become loaves of bread." But he answered, "It is written, 'Man shall not live by bread alone, but by every word that proceeds from the mouth of God.'"

Mt 4:1-4

A natural and correct question that may come to mind: Could someone cognizant of the whole of Creation be tempted into seeing illusion? The answer, of course, is no! Here again we see it was not "the Christ" (a Consciousness beyond limited thought) being tempted, but *the man.* As one develops the ability to discern the different states, it will become apparent that the mind of Man must go through a cleansing of all false beliefs before becoming One with the mind of Christ. This applied to Jesus as well.

By his response to temptation, Jesus professed his faith in a Higher Reality. Jesus knew that **True Reality** existed beyond the limits of the physical world. This belief became so strong that he allowed men to crucify him, thereby revealing that his essence was not limited to the physical body.

> **True, or Ultimate, Reality**
> That which exists beyond the veil of Illusion.

Jesus was representative of the Way, not because he was created differently from anyone else, but because he fully surrendered his attachment to the world of Man in order to obtain something much greater. Once this choice is made and acted upon, Reality will present a different picture. In fact, it is only after one has made the commitment to surrender this world that the Light of Truth shines forth.

Further indication that Jesus placed everyone on the same level as himself can be found in Matthew 5:14 ("You are the light of the world"), where Jesus states to his followers that they are in fact comprised of the same essence (light) as he is.

The eye is the lamp of the body. So, if your eye is
sound, your whole body will be full of light; but if
your eye is not sound, your whole body will be full
of darkness. If then the light in you is darkness,
how great is the darkness!

                                                    Mt 6:22-23

While expanded in Oneness, Jesus remembered his real
essence. He was truly free in those moments. But there were other
times when his human mind (based on perception) caused him
distress. It was at these times of struggle that Jesus found it
necessary to remove himself from the company of others. He would
do this in order to raise his vibration level up to the level of Spirit,
through prayer and meditation.

When Jesus struggled, he revealed his humanness,
demonstrating that he did indeed have an Ego. That Jesus found it
necessary to re-connect testifies to the fact that he was not exempt
from dealing with Original Sin (the mind of Man). The difference
between Jesus and other men was that he demonstrated that this
world could be overcome; in fact, he did overcome it.

I have said this to you, that in me you may have
peace. In the world you have tribulation; but be of
good cheer, I have overcome the world.
                                                    Jn 16:33

Thus, Jesus became the perfect example for anyone to
emulate. It is for you to choose: to live your life with his elevated
state of Consciousness, or to continue your experience in Hell.

And do not fear those who kill the body but cannot
kill the soul; rather fear him who can destroy both
soul and body in hell.
                                                    Mt 10:28

Christ began by teaching the initial steps, the foundation
upon which the understanding of Unconditional Love is built. When
asked where to begin, he instructed men to live righteously, and to

follow the Commandments as a guide for human life.

The Commandments are only necessary to guide you until you develop your awareness to a greater Reality. If there was one thing that set Jesus apart from others, it was his awareness of the greater Self that exists beyond the material. Everything in this world has the potential to pull your attention and keep you from seeing beyond it. That is why Jesus, like other masters, taught us to live without attachments.

When you come to the realization that you are not of this world, but rather one with Christ, everything takes on a new meaning. It is at those times that you are capable of doing anything that Jesus did. Until then, however, you will remain limited and tied to the world; you will be under its law.

> *Truly, truly, I say to you, he who believes in me will also do the works that I do; and greater works than these will he do, because I go to the Father.*
>
> Jn 14:12

What is God?

By this time, I hope that you have begun to understand that your real essence is not physical but rather **Consciousness**, or Spirit. Spirit, by its very nature, is formless. Until this is accepted, there

---
Consciousness

That which pertains to Awareness, both in the human sense and in the spiritual.

---

will be a constant struggle to avoid seeing things in terms of Form. Releasing all concepts of Form is essential to grasping the full meaning of the message of Christ.

In the Gospel of John, Jesus reminds us that God is formless and beyond definition:

> *God is spirit, and those who worship him must worship in spirit and truth.*
>
> Jn 4:24

Now let us go back to the Ten Commandments in the Old Testament, and see if things are beginning to make more sense.

You shall have no other gods before me.

Ex 20:3

While this is the most important of all the Commandments, it is also the most misunderstood—especially by those who think it refers to worshiping Jesus Christ as your God. When you consider that Moses was given the Ten Commandments some 1400 years before the birth of Christ, you can see that having "no gods before me" means to see God as God and not to worship idols of any kind. Limiting yourself to worshiping only a part of God is like having a god before God. God is not any one thing; God is the *totality of the whole*, everything and everyone that exists.

This means that, at their core level (that of Spirit), there is no difference between Jesus, Buddha, Confucius, or the man who just stabbed you in the back. This is hard for most people to accept, because most people are not living in the fullness of Spirit but are living for the personal self.

There exist degrees or levels of awareness of Higher Truth. In this world, as in other dimensions, there is a hierarchy which is directly related to the acceptance of Love (God) over Self. Jesus touched upon this hierarchy when his disciples asked him which of them was best:

Truly, I say to you, among those born of women there has risen no one greater than John the Baptist; yet he who is least in the kingdom of heaven is greater than he.

Mt 11:11

Most people have not even begun to see what is true within this world, much less understand Heaven. This is because they have been conditioned to think that they are already living the highest Truth. In order to move beyond this world, you must be prepared to forego everything here, and replace your attachments with an Unconditional Love for God.

The Matrix of Creation

This world was created by God for Man, in order that he may experience and unfold in Consciousness.

At times, you may find that your Ego will try to delude you into believing that you are living for God. Your creations are not always what you see in your mind, but rather the manifestations of what is in your heart. Jesus spoke of this simple Truth many times; unfortunately, Man is yet unable to fully comprehend what he meant.

In the following passage, where Jesus is speaking to his apostles, he clearly states that every Soul is a creator and is responsible for what it creates.

> *And he said to them, "Then are you also without understanding? Do you not see that whatever goes into a man from outside cannot defile him, since it enters, not his heart but his stomach, and so passes on?" (Thus he declared all foods clean.) And he said, "What comes out of a man is what defiles a man. For from within, out of the heart of man, come evil thoughts, fornication, theft, murder, adultery, coveting, wickedness, deceit, licentiousness, envy, slander, pride, foolishness. All these evil things come from within, and they defile a man."*

Mk 7:18-23

The more one comprehends the words of the Christ, the more one comprehends that within Creation there are levels of awareness, experienced by Soul. Each of these levels exists as different frequencies, in turn interconnected through an intricate matrix.

This matrix is composed of electromagnetic energy, adjusting to everyone's choice to accept Oneness over Separation. In fact, if you were able to behold Ultimate Reality, you would discover that every experience is relative to it, including every experience you have ever had. All experience is based on your thoughts and words—even those you truly do not mean. Each has an energy that must be accounted for. Remember that "You are gods" (Ps 82:6; Jn 10:34). This means that you are responsible for the energy that sets the stage for all that you experience.

> *I tell you, on the day of judgment men will render account for every careless word they utter.*
>
> Mt 12:36

Some might ask: If this is so, then why does it seem that the entire world is blind to it? I would reply that, although the premise is simple, actualizing the experiencing of it is another matter. Our brother Jesus spoke many times of having the "eyes to see." In this world, confusion derives from looking at things through the eyes of Man instead of the eyes of Spirit. The eyes of Man are based on Illusion (perception stemming from Judgment), and the eyes of Spirit are based on Reality (witness to Love without Judgment).

This dichotomy will remain as long as the Ego (the human mind) believes it is in charge of your experiences. In order to move beyond this confusion, you must constantly remind yourself that your Real or true nature is not the human mind, but something far greater and much more powerful. I am referring to a Consciousness that exists beyond time and space.

Although this state is unfamiliar to almost all people, it is actually your authentic nature! It awaits your discovery. It is only after such a discovery that the fullness of life is realized. And until such time that you discover and explore the inner realms of Creation—where you will be awakened to your Higher Self—you will continue to experience only a minuscule piece of What Is.

The difference between these states of Consciousness is so great that Jesus remarked upon it in the Gospel of Thomas:

> *When you know yourselves, then you will be known, and you will know that you are the sons of the living Father. But if you do not know yourselves, then you are in poverty, and you are poverty.*

Thom 3

While some people spend their entire lives exercising and developing their human minds, they tend to overlook the fact that there is a far greater part of Self, i.e., *Consciousness.* This kind of thinking has left them in poverty, so to speak, with a perspective so limited that they can experience only a restricted fragment of What Is. They are like a bodybuilder who focuses all his attention on one muscle and neglects the rest of the body; he is "out of proportion"

| **Higher Self** |
| That part of Soul that identifies with the Spiritual realms. |

indeed! It is of paramount importance to distinguish between Ego (the human self) and the **Higher Self** (Spirit). For those who have eyes to see, the human being is "out of proportion," and in need of a major shift in focus.

This switching from human eyes to spiritual ones is the easiest, as well as the most difficult, thing you can do. Easy, because when you surrender the moment to Spirit you are free from the outcome and are not responsible to work out the details of current perceived problems; difficult, because the switching away from human eyes involves going against what your rational mind is telling you to do. In other words, you must let go of what is perceived—and trust in the unknown.

You are a Spiritual Being, Having a Human Experience

From that time Jesus began to preach, saying, "Repent, for the kingdom of heaven is at hand."

Mt 4:17

Throughout the Bible, there are clues that Time is always a relative thing, a manifested experience within this world. By manifested experience, I do not mean to suggest that the experiences you have "in time" are in any way Absolute Reality. Nor am I implying that such experiences are not real. What I am saying is that there is a Higher Reality existing in the Spiritual world in each moment, a Reality transcending the one perceived as the human experience.

Depending on your level of Awareness, you may or may not be able to discern these different states of conscious experience. Focusing on one does not negate the fact that the other is there, to be experienced.

In this book, I assert that all of Creation based on and existing in Linear Time is an illusion in terms of Ultimate Reality. I would add that the experiencing of the illusion of time can continue for all of eternity.

I realize that this sounds contradictory at first. I can only say that, once human eyes have been replaced with inner or spiritual eyes, all contradiction resulting from the simultaneous existence of both of these states will disintegrate. This change or shift can only come about after a choice. This is why you *must choose* which condition is to be embraced as *your* experience. When considering this choice, it may be helpful to remember that the human experience is limited to perception, while the Spiritual experience not only transcends this limitation but also opens the door to an infinite number of probabilities, all of which exist outside of the realm of time.

This is beyond the scope of the Human mind, as it exists beyond the boundaries of time and space. Whenever the Now is talked about or described, there is always a degree of limitation incorporated in the description. This stems from the fact that all words are limited to Form, and that which is Formless is beyond limitation. It is only in the *Now* (the ever-present moment) that are you capable of experiencing Actual or Absolute Reality.

When Jesus declared that the Kingdom of Heaven is at hand, he was correct. From his level of understanding, it was at hand two thousand years ago, just as it is at hand this year and will be at hand in the year 3000. "Now" always refers to the present moment. Many are familiar with the statement, "Tomorrow never comes." This is a verifiable statement. It can be experienced by anyone— because *Now* always is!

In the following passage from the Gospel of Thomas, Jesus acknowledges a difference between levels of awareness. There was a gap between what he knew as Reality and what his disciples perceived as real.

> *His disciples said to him: On what day will the kingdom come? Jesus said: It will not come while people watch for it; they will not say: Look, here it is, or: Look, there it is; but the kingdom of the father is spread out over the earth, and men do not see it.*
>
> Thom 113

What is Real? What is Illusion?

Who can tell you what is real and what is illusion? Jesus came for that very purpose. His life was a living example of Truth. If you search the Scriptures, you will find that Jesus taught the eternal Truth, the Truth that existed prior to that time, is now, and continues into the future. The difference was Jesus was not just saying the words—he was living and teaching Consciousness.

To live in this world while maintaining your Awareness—this is the re-birthing that Jesus taught to his disciples. While praying to the Father, he declared that they were no longer of the world; they now understood the bigger picture.

> *I have given them thy word; and the world has hated them because they are* not *of the world, even as I am* not *of the world.*
>
> Jn 17:14

For many this Truth is hard to accept, because Ego is quite proficient at creating illusion and will continue to do so for as long as you give it control over your life. There is only one way to work toward having all the experiences necessary to elevate yourself beyond this world: you must become a conscious creator and choose Higher Self over Ego!

> *Then the disciples came and said to him, "Why do you speak to them in parables?" And he answered them, "To you it has been given to know the secrets of the kingdom of heaven, but to them it has not been given. For to him who has will more be given, and he will have abundance; but from him who has not, even what he has will be taken away. This is why I speak to them in parables, because seeing they do not see, and hearing they do not hear, nor do they understand."*
>
> Mt 13:10-13

Why would the truth of God and the mysteries of the Kingdom of Heaven not be for everyone? The Truth is for everyone, but experiences are necessary for the evolution of your Consciousness. Each Soul must experience in order to remember. It is through your remembering that you will unveil the false self and come into the realization that you are Soul!

Man's perception and Jesus' understanding of Truth are worlds apart. Most people are aware that Jesus came into this world to bring peace and love. What they do not accept is that those who hold to this world as their Reality do not understand the peace Jesus came into this world to share.

> *Do not think that I have come to bring peace on earth; I have not come to bring peace, but a sword. For I have come to set a man against his father, and a daughter against her mother, and a daughter-in-law against her mother-in-law; and a man's foes will be those of his own household.*

> Mt 10:34-36

The sword represents cutting through ties to the tribal belief systems that were imposed on you by others. We are not here to adjust our Truth for anyone. In a world based on distortions and false images, you must have the conviction to stand alone, in your Truth, even if this means living in direct opposition to those you love.

Living in the Moment

In the Gospel according to Thomas, the followers of Jesus asked him about their fate: "Tell us how our end will be." Jesus, seeking to open their eyes beyond the limited sight of Man, answered with a question:

> *Since you have discovered the beginning, why do you seek the end? For where the beginning is, there will the end be. Blessed is he who shall stand at the beginning (in the beginning), and he shall know the end, and shall not taste death.*
> Thom 18

Life and death, beginning and end, will always remain confusing labels to the human mind. Until one has moved beyond the limitation of perception, these terms will remain ambiguous, and relative to every individual. Anyone focused on perceptual evidence for his basis of Reality will always experience something related to a past memory. As stated in the Introduction, the human mind is extremely limited in its ability to understand anything that cannot be applied to linear movement. Whenever the human mind tries to conceive of something nonlinear, it is always at a loss.

A personal example: For some time I heard Spirit (God) telling me to stop thinking and just Be. At first, the whole idea confused me each time I heard it; but like anything else, if you are exposed to something often enough it inevitably becomes clearer. After years of meditation and prayer, I came to realize that I was being asked to experience the *Now* moment which transcends the world of normal thought.

Einstein expressed his understanding of this state, existing beyond time and space, when he spoke of the death of a friend.

> *Now he has departed from this strange world a little ahead of me. That means nothing. People like us, who believe in physics, know that the distinction between past, present and future is* only a stubbornly persistent illusion.

Could it be that, over two thousand years ago, Jesus was also aware of this stubbornly persistent illusion? Could it be that time is not limited to the restrictions accepted by Man? When you allow that Dimensions exist far beyond the reach of our self-imposed limitations, you open the door to experience other realms of Creation.

> *In my Father's house are many rooms; if it were not so, would I have told you that I go to prepare a place for you?*
>
> Jn 14:2

When you realize that it was from this level of Consciousness (the position of no time) that Jesus spoke, the statement takes on a different meaning. In fact, in order to comprehend this answer, a change of positional thinking—from that of Man to that of Spirit—is necessary. That was the very reason Jesus answered as he did.

The switch I am referring to here is not easily accepted. Many people will not even accept that there are worlds (dimensions) waiting to be explored, because they cannot accept what the human eye cannot see. This does not mean, however, that there are not many different dimensions awaiting your exploration. The senses are a major obstacle to experiencing beyond the realm of the 3D world. If something cannot be seen, felt, tasted, or smelled most would say it does not exist.

> *"A change of positional thinking—from that of Man to that of Spirit—is necessary."*

As Einstein once said, the mind must change in order to bring about a different experience. The first step in opening the door to a greater level of experience is allowing for the possibility that there is something more than what is familiar. Just because you have no conscious recollection of something does not mean that it cannot exist. When you decide to allow for a greater experience, you will discover that there is much more to see.

> *If I have told you earthly things and you do not believe, how can you believe if I tell you heavenly things? No one has ascended into heaven but he who descended from heaven, the Son of man.*
>
> Jn 3:12-13

Here you see Jesus was clearly asserting that Life existed before the human experience, and that after the human experience is mastered one is reborn. There is a returning to the place of origin, even for the Son of Man.

The Way to Reality

The speaker in Ecclesiastes (Old Testament) noted confusion in understanding the perceived world and the Real world.

> *And I applied my mind to seek and to search out by wisdom all that is done under heaven; it is an unhappy business that God has given to the sons of men to be busy with.*
>
> Eccles 1:13

This speaker has been titled by some "The Teacher." Others suggest that he was King Solomon. Regardless of how you wish to label him, one thing is clear: he saw things differently from most people. In the passage quoted above, it can be seen that he is presenting a message, later amplified by Jesus, about forsaking the illusory world for the real one. He also makes it clear that this process is not without struggle.

The "unhappy business" is not a prerequisite. It is, however, the path many find themselves walking upon. Attachment to the Form, or what most people have as their "take on reality," is what Jesus referred to as poverty.

There is a way out of this state of poverty, but it does not come without pitfalls. Within the human experience, most will find there are many obstacles that stand in the way. They prevent one from seeing the light that already exists. The amount of light (true vision) that gets through determines the amount of perceived pain associated with this world. Although the pain may be based wholly on illusion, while suffering it you are having a real experience.

The degree of pain associated with overcoming this illusory experience is, therefore, up to each individual. It can be minimized; when the Attachment to Form is released, the suffering goes with it.

The Return to Life/Love

As our story unfolds, you can observe that there is indeed a succession or expanding of Awareness for Man. This is called Evolution. From the time of what appeared to be total ignorance, we find Man muddling his way along, groping in the dark, struggling to recover the Light that was lost. According to the Old Testament, a Savior or Messiah was to come to restore Life, or to restore sight to the blind. (This involves the figurative meaning of *sight*, of course. As explained previously, the human mind has a propensity to interpret words only to fit into the perceived world.)

It is this limited perception that maintains that Veil of Illusion accepted by most as real. The sad truth is, however, as long as one embraces the limited (finite) over the unlimited (infinite), one remains blinded to a greater Reality.

> *Jesus said: Recognize what is before you, and what is hidden from you will be revealed to you; for there is nothing hidden that will not be made manifest.*
>
> Thom 5

It has been said that Satan's greatest trick is to convince Man that he doesn't exist. Here again we are faced with a truth that is clouded in misunderstanding. Satan, like Ego, is another metaphor for a state of Consciousness. In the section on Time and Energy, we will look more closely at this, but for now it is enough to say that Satan is synonymous with the vibration of Fear. There are a few Bible sayings that aid in understanding:

God is love

There is no fear in love

God is that which never changes

Examined separately, each of these tenets is a powerful assertion; when you combine the three, you have a powerful precept, one that is essential to removing the veil of illusion from the eyes of Man. On the one hand there is God (Love), and on the other hand Satan (Fear).

The Illusion of Death

While attempting to see (understand) Truth, it is beneficial to note that it was through errors in judgment that the Death Experience came about in the first place. Death has no reality in and of itself, nor does it truly exist outside of the mind of Man. Within the realm of Creation as God intended it, death is impossible. Indeed, it is contrary to Creation itself...

> *For as by a man came death, by a man has come*
> *also the resurrection of the dead.*

1 Cor 15:21

A basic understanding of this is essential to anyone who wishes to experience Ultimate Reality (where death does not exist). Man's belief in death brought the experience into Form; once that belief is changed, the experience will end. Another way to put it would be to say that, just because something is experienced in this world, it is not Absolute Reality. Within Absolute Reality exist an infinite number of perceived realities. Each perceived reality is real to the perceiver, but only as a *perceived* experience.

In the world of Man's perceived experiences, one thing is certain: given enough time and exposure, change is inevitable. New ways of seeing things continually arise. This is true because Form (i.e., that which becomes manifest to be experienced) is always a result of thought, based on beliefs. Change the mind and the belief is changed. This will bring about a change in the way of experience.

The Illusion of the Ego's Perceptual World

Later I will address the fact that there is perfection in each moment, relative to the choices you make. Despite this, there is a greater experience available: you may choose to change the meaning you have given to the circumstances surrounding your life. If this sounds confusing it is only because you have an erroneous assumption built on your past emotions or beliefs.

As long as your mind is tied to past patterns of thoughts (beliefs tied to memories), you will forever re-experience the same distortions. These distortions will block your way to an understanding of the nature of Consciousness itself (God). The responsibility of this all-important job cannot be left to another. Only you are capable of calling forth any experience, including awakening to your True Self. Heaven is at hand right in front of you, but you must focus with a new set of eyes to see it. The veil must be removed by the one who maintains it.

In this world of Time, there has been an evolution of Consciousness, and little by little, Man has evolved his limited mind to prepare for his re-connecting. Here is an example from the New Testament. In the Sermon on the Mount, Jesus assures the people that he does not intend to take away what they believe, but wants to add to their understanding by introducing the power of thought.

> *Think not that I have come to abolish the law and the prophets; I have come not to abolish them but to fulfill them. For truly, I say to you, till heaven and earth pass away, not an iota, not a dot, will pass from the law until all is accomplished. Whoever then relaxes one of the least of these commandments and teaches men so, shall be called least in the kingdom of heaven; but he who does them and teaches them shall be called great in the kingdom of heaven. For I tell you, unless your righteousness exceeds that of the scribes and Pharisees, you will never enter the kingdom of heaven. You have heard that it was said to the men of old, 'You shall not kill; and whoever kills shall be liable to judgment.' But I say to you that every one who is angry with his brother shall be liable to judgment; whoever insults his brother shall be liable to the council, and whoever says, 'You fool!' shall be liable to the hell of fire. So if you are offering your gift at the altar, and there remember that your brother has something against you, leave*

your gift there before the altar and go; first be reconciled to your brother, and then come and offer your gift.

Mt 5:17-24

Know Yourself

In the first parts of the Gospel of Thomas, Jesus points out the need for understanding. He starts off with the assertion that, in order to move back into Life, one must understand the real meaning of his words. This ability to discern his message comes to anyone who sees through the eyes of Love (Non-Judgment).

And he said: He who shall find the interpretation of these words shall not taste of death.

Thom 1

Jesus said: He who seeks, let him not cease seeking until he finds; and when he finds he will be troubled, and when he is troubled he will be amazed, and he will reign over the All.

Thom 2

Jesus said: If those who lead you say to you: See, the kingdom is in heaven, then the birds of the heaven will go before you; if they say to you: It is in the sea, then the fish will go before you. But the kingdom is within you, and it is outside of you. When you know yourselves, then you will be known, and you will know that you are the sons of the living Father. But if you do not know yourselves, then you are in poverty, and you are poverty.

Thom 3

What does it mean to know yourself, and why did Jesus stress this point?

Up to the time of Jesus, focus was on the outer man, and great emphasis was placed on following the Law. The Law required everyone to become a good Ego (human). In this world, it is certainly better to be "good" as opposed to "bad," and if this is our home, the best we could hope for is that everyone would become good. This world, however, is not your home but a school—a school that prepares you for your real home.

Many have formed such an attachment to the physical world that they have no conscious recollection of their real essence as Spirit. To truly interpret the words of Christ, or any other master who speaks of Unconditional Love, requires you to connect to the vibration of Love. This can occur only through Non-Judgment.

One must go within oneself, connecting with the Higher Mind that is Spirit. Otherwise, the mind that caused the confused state is the same mind that is trying to find the answers. Then you will always see the same distorted view, the one that only appears to be real.

Jesus was certain that there were many people who, try as they might, could hear all his words and obtain nothing except confusion. There are those who feel they can intellectualize their way to understanding, but this will always prove to be a fruitless effort. The Reality of Oneness/Love cannot be intellectualized—it can only be experienced.

> *A person starts to live when he can live outside of himself.*

> Albert Einstein

Again, in the Gospel of Thomas, Jesus speaks of one such Truth that many will not understand.

> *Blessed is he who shall stand at the beginning (in the beginning), and he shall know the end, and shall not taste death.*

> Thom 18

As it was presented in the Old Testament, the whole illusion of (or belief in) Death started with a choice made by Adam and Eve. This same choice is offered to everyone in every moment. If you go back to the beginning in the Garden, you will find that it is *Judgment* that causes the experience of Separation; this is the real message the Great Master spoke to a deaf world.

You could say, in fact, that the choice given to Adam and Eve is the same choice you face in every moment of every day. Judge any part of Creation and you lose the ability to see the whole of Creation. This, then, is the ULTIMATE CHOICE.

"Heaven is at Hand"

Throughout his ministry, Jesus stated repeatedly, "Heaven is at hand." Not many people fully understand the significance of this statement. However, it was true at the time and is still true today.

Heaven *is* at hand. Right here and right now, you can choose to expand your Consciousness and feel the love of God in everyone and in everything. The only thing that keeps you from this experience is you—or rather, your Ego. God's love does not come into and out of your life. God is as constant as the air that you breathe. You are the one who separates yourself from it.

> If I ascend to heaven, thou art there! If I make my
> bed in hell, thou art there!
>
> Ps 139:8

You cannot hide from God. You only delude yourself when you believe that the Separation you feel is real.

God's Love is impersonal and God never judges your actions. You are always worthy of God's Love, if you believe it to be so or not. It is Unconditional. It is the kind of Love Jesus spoke of when he said, "Love your neighbor as yourself."

When you come to see Truth and recognize yourself as part of God, you must also recognize all Souls as part of God, no different from you. It takes each and every Soul to make up the body of God.

> *Being asked by the Pharisees when the kingdom of*
> *God was coming, he answered them, "The kingdom*
> *of God is not coming with signs to be observed; nor*
> *will they say, 'Lo, here it is!' or 'There!' for behold,*
> *the kingdom of God is in the midst of you."*
>
> Lk 17:20-21

The Kingdom of God is in everyone; nevertheless, in order to perceive it, you must accept it. Whatever you fully accept as a valid truth will be a real experience to you. The very moment you feel doubt, you will shift from Love to Fear and become blinded to the Truth.

You Are the Creators

> *Enter by the narrow gate; for the gate is wide and*
> *the way is easy, that leads to destruction, and those*
> *who enter by it are many. For the gate is narrow*
> *and the way is hard, that leads to life, and those*
> *who find it are few.*
>
> Mt 7:13-14

If you think that all you have to do is believe in Jesus Christ and you will go to heaven, you are going to be greatly disappointed. This idea cannot be further from the truth.

It is your responsibility to remember you have Free Will. This means that you always have choices to make in every moment. You must live with the Consciousness that Jesus spoke of, before you move through the gate to salvation. The gate will always be open to you, but it will always be your choice to enter. You choose whether you live for God or not.

> *Not every one who says to me, 'Lord, Lord,' shall enter the kingdom of heaven, but he who does the will of my Father who is in heaven. On that day many will say to me, 'Lord, Lord, did we not prophesy in your name, and cast out demons in your name, and do many mighty works in your name?' And then will I declare to them, 'I never knew you; depart from me, you evildoers.'*
>
> Mt 7:21-23

You will say, "Lord, I have prophesied in your name," and Jesus will say he never knew you. How is it possible that, even when you have been doing the work of the Lord, Jesus would deny you? The truth is, Jesus is not the one who denies you; it is *you* who choose Ego over Higher Self.

> *And I tell you, Ask, and it will be given you; seek, and you will find; knock, and it will be opened to you.*
>
> Lk 11:9

Salvation comes only to those who seek it. Asking is only the beginning, knocking opens the door, but the experience only comes to those who walk through the door.

Christ as the Savior

Like many before him, Jesus was greatly misunderstood by the majority of those who heard his words. Of all these misunderstandings, the greatest concerned his role as Savior, and the meaning of this for the people of the world.

Was he actually the Savior of Man? Did his death on the cross wash away every sin that has been committed, before or since? The answer to these questions is both yes and no—and the only way to clear up this confusion is to remove the veil of **Judgment** that is obscuring true vision.

> **Judgment**
> Evaluating something based on a system of Duality, i.e. Good versus Evil. That which precludes an outcome.

Here is the foundation for true salvation. The only thing that stands in the way of it is the veil of ignorance.

Confusion over this point has led to teaching dogma as opposed to Truth. Jesus did not die for your sins so you could live in denial and be absolved of responsibility for your own salvation. Rather, he came here to become the way-shower to Truth and Life. The Real Truth Jesus spoke of was one of personal responsibility. Each one of us is responsible for his own experience.

As a Christian, I was taught that to think of myself first was a selfish thing. In fact, Jesus taught the exact opposite. Whenever you are thinking of your Spiritual Self, you are transcending the process of the human mind; this is the most unselfish thing anyone can offer to the rest of Mankind. When asked how he could abandon his wife and child forever to seek enlightenment, the Buddha answered that it was because he loved mankind and wanted to relieve it of all pain and suffering.

Jesus taught this same kind of Love:

> *Greater love has no man than this, that a man lay down his life for his friends.*

> Jn 15:13

The Truth of Salvation

Many are convinced that what they believe in is the Absolute Truth of Jesus. Many will use Biblical quotes to support their positions, even when those positions are clearly Ego-based and from the mind of Man. Each person must decide what level of Truth is for him or her. That is what Free Will is all about. Those who wish to experience the joy of Oneness again must look to the highest level of Truth, and settle for nothing less than Ultimate Reality.

In the Gospel of Thomas, Jesus asks for nothing less than Total Awareness:

> *Jesus said: He who seeks, let him not cease seeking until he finds; and when he finds he will be troubled, and when he is troubled he will be amazed, and he will reign over the All.*

> Thom 2

The highest Truth Jesus spoke of was Non-Judgment (Unconditional Love), where sin does not exist. Jesus stressed this state as the final objective for Man and the way to Eternal Life. He alluded to this level of Truth when he said:

> *And you will know the Truth, and the Truth will make you free.*

> Jn 8:32

If you can learn to see with your Spiritual Eyes as apposed to interpreting every word with your limited mind, this Truth becomes indisputable. It is at this time that you will awaken from the dream containing the illusion of the Death Experience. Once this is accomplished, you will lose all attachment to the Form you previously believed was life. In that moment, you will be transformed into the state Jesus was referring to when he spoke of overcoming Death. This is the true meaning of becoming reborn.

> *I know your works: you are neither cold nor hot. Would that you were cold or hot! So, because you are lukewarm, and neither cold nor hot, I will spew you out of my mouth. For you say, I am rich, I have prospered, and I need nothing; not knowing that you are wretched, pitiable, poor, blind, and naked. Therefore I counsel you to buy from me gold refined by fire, that you may be rich, and white garments*

*to clothe you and to keep the shame of your
nakedness from being seen, and salve to anoint
your eyes, that you may see. Those whom I love, I
reprove and chasten; so be zealous and repent.
Behold, I stand at the door and knock; if any one
hears my voice and opens the door, I will come in
to him and eat with him, and he with me. He who
conquers, I will grant him to sit with me on my
throne, as I myself conquered and sat down with
my Father on his throne.*

Rev 3:15-21

By the term "conquer," Jesus meant the overcoming of your
Ego, or judgmental mind.

Judgment

This world is full of Judgment. Take a moment to ask yourself if
you have any Judgment of anyone or anything.

The truth is that God never judges us. Judgment exists only
within our own Consciousness. It originates in the mind and comes
from past beliefs. It is not instinctive. If you have thoughts of
Judgment, you will live that creation. When you choose not to
judge, Judgment is not in your reality. It is as simple as that.

There are many references to judgment in the Bible. Here are
just a few:

*Jesus said, "For judgment I came into this world,
that those who do not see may see, and that those
who see may become blind."*

Jn 9:39

Jesus came here to bring in an understanding of
Consciousness to all willing to see. "Those who see" refers to those
who falsely thought they were living the Truth; they shall be made
blind to their misconceptions.

The Father judges no one, but has given all judgment to the Son.

Jn 5:22

God gave Man Free Will. All Creation takes on its own movement within a perfect interplay of energy. It is impossible for God or anyone else to judge your thoughts or your creations. This does not mean, however, that there is no consequence for the thoughts or actions that originate in your judgmental mind.

"All judgment to the Son" refers to how Soul judges itself relative to perfect Love. As you move through this world or the worlds to come, you will always be faced with the consequences of your thoughts (judgments). As long as you remain connected to this world by your thoughts, you will be subject to the law of Karma.

You judge according to the flesh, I judge no one.

Jn 8:15

Do not think that I shall accuse you to the Father; it is Moses who accuses you, on whom you set your hope.

Jn 5:45

If any one hears my sayings and does not keep them, I do not judge him; for I did not come to judge the world but to save the world.

Jn 12:47

Again, Jesus' message was for Man to understand what it means to elevate his Consciousness beyond this world. You can see from these verses that if you do not judge anyone, including yourself, you will be free from the consequences of your judgment.

For with the judgment you pronounce you will be judged, and the measure you give will be the measure you get.

Mt 7:2

*I tell you, on the day of judgment men will render
account for every careless word they utter.*

Mt 12:36

It is important not to confuse
Judgment with discernment. You have full
responsibility for your every thought and
action. Every one of your thoughts will
contribute to your experiences, as well as
affecting the experiences of others through
the **Collective Consciousness**.

> **Collective Consciousness**
> The sum of Energy produced by the Genuine Will of all persons present in this world.

*And if any one will not receive you or listen to your
words, shake off the dust from your feet as you
leave that house or town. Truly, I say to you, it
shall be more tolerable on the day of judgment for
the land of Sodom and Gomorrah than for that
town.*

Mt 10:14-15

Jesus was saying that, when you speak Truth and your
listeners choose to remain in their Ego minds, you are to walk away
and let them remain lost in their illusions. They are going to have to
live the consequences of their creations—just as you will have to
live yours.

Before moving on, I would like to return once again to an
important point. Many are still confused by the meaning of
accepting Jesus as Savior. To be saved does not negate or lessen the
personal responsibility that is at the core of Free Will. Merely
accepting that Jesus died for Man's sins does not overcome the
effects of the laws of this world. Many people will be greatly
disappointed to find that they were wrong to make such an
assumption.

At some point, all will come to understand that there is no judge to condemn or promote anyone. All experience within Creation is the result of choices made by each individual. Later we shall look at the will of the Father as opposed to the will of Man, but for now let it suffice to say that the option is always there to choose one over the other. This is the principle of Free Will. Free Will simply means that everyone is given the choice to experience himself as Spirit (free of the Law of Man), or to remain in bondage to the elements of the world as seen by human eyes.

Lifting the Veil

But their minds were hardened; for to this day, when they read the old covenant, that same veil remains unlifted, because only through Christ is it taken away. Yes, to this day whenever Moses is read a veil lies over their minds...

2 Cor 3:14-16

Here we see that the veil upon the mind of Man remained even when the words of Moses were read. This is because Moses was teaching the way of Man and Jesus was taking things to a higher level, that of Spirit.

If you follow the stories of the Old Testament, you will find that people were in great need of guidance. Hence the Law. This Law, however, was not designed to bring back the vision of Man in order to remember the Oneness. It was to be a guide and a tool for teaching mankind how to live in a world of Separation (the Death Experience). Their attachment to the belief that this physical world is real is what is meant by the "veil over their minds."

Fear is a direct by-product of a thought system rooted in the physical. This is because nothing in the physical universe is permanent. Fear is the measure for Judgment in this world. While using this standard you will always find support for your convictions, because the majority of the people are suffering from the same delusions. Once you discern Real Truth, you will most likely be seen by the world as a fool.

> *The unspiritual man does not receive the gifts of the Spirit of God, for they are folly to him, and he is not able to understand them because they are spiritually discerned.*
>
> 1 Cor 2:14

The "unspiritual man" refers to those who have an attachment to the human experience, which sees things only in terms of relevance to this world.

> *Let no one deceive himself. If any one among you thinks that he is wise in this age, let him become a fool that he may become wise. For the wisdom of this world is folly with God. For it is written, "He catches the wise in their craftiness."*
>
> 1 Cor 3:18-19

Here we see a distinction between the states of consciousness accessible through choice. At times, it may appear that you do not have a choice as to the level of awareness you experience, because of the veil that clouds your vision. This veil represents the distorted beliefs held as reality, within a judgmental human mind. It is important to remember that the veil exists relative to your beliefs; *you* are the one who maintains the veil. You will either see True Reality, or maintain your own perceptual dream where light cannot penetrate.

To sum up, then: Moses had the job of introducing the Law to guide Man while in the world of Separation/Judgment (i.e., the dream). This Law showed Man how to become morally righteous (good humans). Jesus, on the other hand, came here to teach Man how to reconnect with the Higher Reality and move out of the world of Separation.

...but when a man turns to the Lord the veil is removed. Now the Lord is the Spirit, and where the Spirit of the Lord is, there is freedom. And we all, with unveiled face, beholding the glory of the Lord, are being changed into his likeness from one degree of glory to another; for this comes from the Lord who is the Spirit.

2 Cor 3:16-18

As you turn away from your attachments to this world, you begin to see True Reality, as the veil is removed from your eyes. The change that takes place happens not as one complete moment but in degrees. This re-birthing process comes from a choice that must be repeatedly renewed. When Jesus said that the greatest gift you can give is to lay down your life for your fellow man, this is what he was referring to. He also said that it is possible to pick it up again. Such a choice would "restore the veil."

Whenever you honor your humanness over the Higher (Spiritual) Self, you are in fact forsaking your Spiritual Self for your human self. Your mind will be blinded thereby.

Non-Judgment: The Key to Removing the Veil

Vibration
Rate of frequency of energy, including thought.

As long as you are judging yourself or another, you are not in the **Vibration** of Love and it is impossible to consciously experience the Now Moment. Everyone who has attained the level of awareness of the Now shares one characteristic: he has overcome the habitual practice of Judgment. With time, you will discover that this is the answer to all (perceived) problems that distract you. Many would have you believe that it is your job to work out solutions to the problems in this world, as apposed to discerning that there is a higher way of dealing with each one.

Jesus chastised the Scribes and the Pharisees (teachers of the law) for not teaching the fullness of such truths.

But woe to you, scribes and Pharisees, hypocrites!
because you shut the kingdom of heaven against
men; for you neither enter yourselves, nor allow
those who would enter to go in.

Mt 23:13

You hypocrites! Well did Isaiah prophesy of you,
when he said: "This people honors me with their
lips, but their heart is far from me; in vain do they
worship me, teaching as doctrines the precepts of
men."

Mt 15:7-9

The Scribes and Pharisees mentioned above were guilty of misleading men. They taught that one is to follow the letter of the Law relative to this world only, without teaching them how to overcome it.

There are several well-known passages where Jesus directly addresses the Scribes and Pharisees, and warns them of the harm they are doing by obscuring the truth. His warning was well founded: each person is subject to and responsible for his own thoughts.

According to Jesus, there is a clear need to be pure of heart before prayer. He even goes so far as to point out that it is necessary to clear all judgmental thoughts before offering a gift to the Father. He referred to this because of his understanding of the Law of Attraction. You cannot escape the consequences of your thoughts playing out in this world. This being true, it becomes obvious that by holding onto a judgment about another it is impossible to connect with the vibration of God (an Unconditionally Loving presence).

Make friends quickly with your accuser, while you
are going with him to court, lest your accuser hand
you over to the judge, and the judge to the guard,

and you be put in prison; truly, I say to you, you
will never get out till you have paid the last penny.
                                          Mt 5:25-26

No one escapes the law of cause and effect, and every thought must be accounted for in some way, either by experience or by Grace. I will talk more about Grace as we move along, but for now it is helpful to remember that the events in your life are being perfectly orchestrated to fit the picture *you* have constructed in order to purge yourself of Ego (i.e., the Judgmental Mind).

When referring to the picture you have constructed, I do not mean to imply that you retain in your memory all the details you have contributed with your every thought; but you can rest assured that you gave the Holy Spirit a specific vibration. This occurs so as to bring about each moment of experience in a precise and exact form. Even though most people are blind to the power of their thoughts, they are nonetheless calling forth experiences as lessons, to manifest themselves in every moment.

You have heard that it was said, "You shall not
commit adultery." But I say to you that every one
who looks at a woman lustfully has already
committed adultery with her in his heart.
                                          Mt 5:27-28

Imagine how difficult it would have been for people to accept this notion: lusting after a woman in thought was creating an experience as valid as any witnessed in the physical realm! I daresay that not many today are awake enough to fully understand this concept. Despite this, Jesus emphasized the power of thought and stressed the consequence of misguided focuses.

If your right eye causes you to sin, pluck it out and
throw it away; it is better that you lose one of your
members than that your whole body be thrown into
hell. And if your right hand causes you to sin, cut
it off and throw it away; it is better that you lose

*one of your members than that your whole body go
into hell.*

Mt 5:29-30

You could say no one can circumvent the laws of Creation, or their effects. There is one, and only one, way to change the events in your life: you must take full responsibility for your thoughts. If you imagine this is difficult to do while living in this world, following the desires of a human mind, I would agree with you. Not only is it difficult to do this, but as long as you allow your past to govern your present you will find it impossible to be perfect. It is only when you can realize the experience of Unconditional Love, a love that is all-inclusive, do you experience perfection. Although unfamiliar to most, this state of purity is your natural state: you have never really left it, and it is there for you whenever you are willing to let this world—along with all its attachments—go. It is then that you are truly reborn.

Paul went into a great deal of detail describing the difference between the experience of Spirit as opposed to that of Man. In Romans, he talked of moving above the Law; this would involve ceasing to live in a world of Judgment.

*For Christ is the end of the Law, that every one
who has faith may be justified.*

Rom 10:4

Paul understood that Christ represented a level of Consciousness that did not come from one who was blinded and asleep.

*Besides this you know what hour it is, how it is full
time now for you to wake from sleep. For salvation
is nearer to us now than when we first believed...*

Rom 13:11

Not only did Paul understand that Christ brought salvation to the world by the teaching of Non-Judgment—he took it upon himself to spread the good news.

> *Do not, for the sake of food, destroy the work of God. Everything is indeed clean, but it is wrong for any one to make others fall by what he eats; it is right not to eat meat or drink wine or do anything that makes your brother stumble. The faith that you have, keep between yourself and God; happy is he who has no reason to judge himself for what he approves. But he who has doubts is condemned, if he eats, because he does not act from faith; for whatever does not proceed from faith is sin.*
>
> Rom 14:20-23

Whatever is done while holding on to Judgment will condemn us to experiencing the Law (Karma); what is done in Love (Non-judgment) will bring us peace.

Before moving on, I would like to answer a question I have heard many times regarding non-judgment. Many people (in their human mind) have asked me if I believed that they could do anything to others, as long as they did not judge themselves. The answer to this question is simple: God will not be mocked (Gal 6:7). Although you can pretend to fool yourself into believing that you are not judging, the truth will at some point be revealed.

"The Son referred to by Jesus is your Spiritual Self."

Jesus made a point of saying that the Father will not judge you. He also said that he did not come to judge, but to save. He said all Judgment was of the Son. At the time of your leaving your current physical body, you will find that the Son referred to by Jesus is your Spiritual Self.

Some persons have had what is called "Near-Death Experiences." These people claim to have seen their entire lives somehow flash before their eyes. This can only happen when you are beyond the limits of time and space. Some have had a beautiful experience, while others were terrified with what they saw. The experiences were different because of the different degrees of Love the people were open to.

Those interested in justice will not be disappointed, for there is indeed a divine justice that no one can escape. This justice does not come from a judge, but is rather the consequence of choices we have made. At the time of death, each will face his day of judgment, and each will recognize how close or how far away from perfect Love he truly is. Depending on where he happens to fall on the scale, each will be moved to continue his journey within one of the rooms (dimensions) within the infinite Matrix.

Jesus called this moment the Second Death. (The first was the original death brought about by Judgment in the Garden of Eden.)

> *He who has an ear, let him hear what the Spirit says to the churches. He who conquers shall not be hurt by the second death.*
>
> Rev 2:11

The Reality of Sin

> *So with us; when we were children, we were slaves to the elemental spirits of the universe. But when the time had fully come, God sent forth his Son, born of woman, born under the law, to redeem those who were under the law, so that we might receive adoption as sons. And because you are sons, God has sent the Spirit of his Son into our hearts,*

crying, "Abba! Father!" So through God you are no longer a slave but a son, and if a son then an heir.

Gal 4:3-7

Much can be gained by correctly understanding this passage. Start with the concept of Original Sin: if you refer back to the scene in the Garden of Eden, you can now see that being born with Original Sin is not what is usually taught. This stems from the misleading meaning ascribed to the term *sin*.

Sin, as portrayed by Adam and Eve in the Garden, was the act of going against God's Will. Judging things as Good or Evil sets energy in motion, energy that is rooted in Duality. While you can say that everyone "is born with Original Sin," it means that everyone who lives in this world with the mind of Man is going against God's Will, and is therefore under the Law. Anyone who practices the act of Judgment is, in fact, under the Law of Man and is experiencing the same death (or state of Separation) represented by Adam and Eve. This state will continue until one moves into a level of Consciousness that is capable of transcending it, by opening to a higher experience.

How the World Heard Christ

Understanding what Jesus taught is difficult, to say the least. This is because the normal reaction for most people is to use their experiences in the physical world, including their Ego's agendas and attachments, in a futile attempt to comprehend something that cannot fit into such a limited view.

The sad fact is that Man sees things in a distorted way. If this is not clear to you, perhaps it is because your heart has not opened to the level of love that Jesus taught. Understanding comes to those who have a strong enough desire to develop it; it does not come to everyone, but only to those who are genuinely seeking. Remember how Jesus addressed the religious leaders of the day:

"But woe to you, scribes and Pharisees, hypocrites! because you shut the kingdom of heaven against men; for you neither enter yourselves, nor allow those who would enter to go in."

Mt 23:13

What the scribes taught the people was not the path to Heaven. Jesus pointed out that not only were their teachings erroneous, but the teachers themselves were lost.

Although many saw and felt Truth in the words Jesus spoke, they found it easier to deny it. It was easier for men to see Jesus as a god capable of living a life detached from this world than to recognize him as human. In that way, they could justify their choice to live for Ego and exempt themselves from taking responsibility for their actions and creations.

It is not always easy to live for God. Even those who were in the presence of Jesus had many moments where they chose to live for this world. Ego is very powerful, and not many people are willing to give up their illusions to live for God (Higher Self). This is easily observed when you look at this world. Has the Collective Consciousness been choosing to create from their Egos (Fear) or from their Higher Selves (Love)? Each and every thought, each and every choice, is significant to the whole of creation and affects the world. This world for the most part is not representative of Heaven, but of Hell—because of the choices made by Man.

A Shift in Consciousness

In order to fully experience the kind of peace and love Jesus spoke of, you must be willing to surrender Ego. As you have learned, Ego is that part of Soul that is concerned with this world. It will keep you blinded to the Truth.

Since your experiences are directly related to your perceptions, if you cannot see beyond this world, you will not be able to experience beyond this world. There is only one way to break the cycle of **Karma** and free you from your own mind: once you recognize Truth, it will be impossible for you to ever be separated from God. Within this level of Consciousness, all fears disappear. No longer are you worried about that which is finite, because you now recognize that you, along with every other person, are part of an infinite Creation.

> **Karma**
> The law of Balance. The impersonal system of energy that restores equilibrium to the unbalanced.

You do not need anyone's approval to be One with God. This Truth was what Jesus came here to teach by laying down his life. Until this is accepted, there will be a need for further instruction, not for punishment, but rather for opportunities.

This world was created as a school. It is a place for Soul to unfold and evolve in Consciousness, rediscovering the real meaning of Love. Once this is understood, this world and the things of this world will no longer hold the same meaning for you.

However, there are no guarantees that you will not miss the mark and let sin take over once again. There are many potential traps that Ego uses to keep you locked into the world, blind to higher Truth. While it is true that all things are of God, this world is a playground for Ego.

> *Unfaithful creatures! Do you not know that friendship with the world is enmity with God? Therefore whoever wishes to be a friend of the world makes himself an enemy of God.*
>
> Jas 4:4

This does not mean that you cannot live in this world, once you see through its illusion. When you choose to live in this world for God, you become a co-creator with God. Another way of saying this: You are a conduit that Spirit uses to achieve God's will, in a world driven by Man's will.

Jesus lived in this world, but most of the time he was not of this world in Consciousness. While he remembered his real essence, he held to the larger and true picture.

> *He said to them, "You are from below, I am from above; you are of this world, I am not of this world."*
>
> Jn 8:23

It was only when Jesus forgot that his real home was not of this world that he struggled with attachment to the human Form.

> *And going a little farther he fell on his face and prayed, "My Father, if it be possible, let this cup pass from me; nevertheless, not as I will, but as thou wilt."*
>
> Mt 26:39

This struggle did not last long: Jesus remembered that he did not come here to do his will, but the will of the Father. Contrary to popular belief, Jesus had moments of struggle within himself, and warned mankind that maintaining a connection to Life (God) requires constant effort.

Once you have the understanding that you are responsible for your Reality, you must become vigilant in your choices. As you do, you will view all things as though you are in this world but not of it. This is the real meaning of being reborn.

> *And no one puts new wine into old wineskins; if he does, the wine will burst the skins, and the wine is lost, and so are the skins; but new wine is for fresh skins.*
>
> Mk 2:22

Once you expand your vision, it will not fit into your old bottles. You cannot shrink your new, expanded Consciousness; you have to adjust your lifestyle to your new Consciousness, and be willing to move past anyone or anything that is holding you to your past belief. *You came into this world alone, and you leave this world alone.*

Perception is everything when it comes to Consciousness. As long as you choose to maintain a limited degree of awareness, you will be limited in your vision. It doesn't really matter if it is money, a car, power, or a person; if you have an attachment to anything, you are creating Separation from the Real and holding on to illusion.

Be Not of This World

Jesus talked of two distinct states of Consciousness; one focused on this world, and the other focused on Heaven.

> *I am praying for them; I am not praying for the world but for those whom thou hast given me, for they are thine.*
>
> Jn 17:9

Notice that Jesus was not praying for this world, but for those who he knew had chosen to see beyond this world; for those who had eyes to see, and for those who had ears to hear.

Jesus had a conscious understanding that was not of this world. He saw far beyond the Consciousness of those living here. Because of this, he said things that were hard for us to comprehend.

> *Jesus answered, "My kingship is not of this world; if my kingship were of this world, my servants would fight, that I might not be handed over to the Jews; but my kingship is not from the world."*
>
> Jn 18:36

Jesus recognized that the world was not his place within the Matrix of Creation. Nevertheless, he was here for a purpose. Each person must participate either in serving the will of God (that which serves the whole) or the will of Man (that which serves the personal Self). Once accepted, serving the will of God does not mean that you can no longer live in this world; it means that the experience here changes from self to selfless, or from Man to God.

Imagine for a moment what this world would be like if everyone chose to live his life for God. To live your life for God means to choose consciously, letting go of attachment to all outcomes in every moment. Needless to say, this is contrary to the way of the world. It is the primary reason Jesus asked the Father to look over the ones who accepted his message.

> *I have given them thy word; and the world has hated them because they are not of the world, even as I am not of the world. I do not pray that thou shouldst take them out of the world, but that thou shouldst keep them from the evil one. They are not of the world, even as I am not of the world.*
>
> Jn 17:14-16

Jesus made reference to the fact that those who move beyond this world in Consciousness are no longer of this world. This was his true purpose. He came here so others would be able to find their way home by his example.

If there is one line that sums up what Jesus represented, this is it:

> *Him only shall you serve.*
>
> Mt 4:10

By "him" Jesus was, of course, speaking of God the Father.

Separation

Everyone is taught to accept what is believed to be of value for survival. Nevertheless, there is a great difference between focusing upon worldly things and the Reality of the worlds beyond. In the following verses Jesus explains what occurs if you allow yourself to be caught up in distractions: you risk losing your ability to discern the different states.

They are those who hear the word, but the cares of the world, and the delight in riches, and the desire for other things, enter in and choke the word, and it proves unfruitful.

Mk 4:18-19

Jesus knew that there would always be those who refuse to take responsibility for their lives because of overwhelming attachment to the physical Form. He gave the best advice he could have given at the time: he told them to go back and make friends with the world.

And I tell you, make friends for yourselves by means of unrighteous mammon, so that when it fails they may receive you into the eternal habitations.

Lk 16:9

He gave such advice because you cannot split yourself between two worlds and do justice to either.

No servant can serve two masters; for either he will hate the one and love the other, or he will be devoted to the one and despise the other. You cannot serve God and mammon.

Lk 16:13

It is our attachment to the things of this world that stands in the way of our connectedness.

But he said to them, "You are those who justify yourselves before men, but God knows your hearts;

*for what is exalted among men is an abomination
in the sight of God."*

Lk 16:15

Of all things in the world, Man is most proud of his
intellectual mind. The Bible addresses this, and goes so far as to say
you must become a fool to the world in order to become spiritually
discerning.

*Let no one deceive himself. If any one among you
thinks that he is wise in this age, let him become a
fool that he may become wise.*

1 Cor 3:18

You may have also read that in the "End Times" there will
be many claiming to have come in the name of the Christ. It is at
times difficult to distinguish between those wanting to help and
those who want to control. My only advice would be similar to that
of Mother Theresa, who said:

*In the end you are going to find out that life was
never about them and you, but about you and God.*

With Spiritual Eyes

*Jesus said: If you do not fast to the world, you will
not find the kingdom; if you do not keep the
Sabbath as Sabbath, you will not see the Father.*

Thom 27

*Jesus said: I stood in the midst of the world, and I
appeared to them in the flesh. I found them all
drunk; I found none of them thirsting, and my soul
was afflicted for the sons of men; for they are blind
in their heart, and they do not see that they came
empty into the world, (and) empty they seek to
leave the world again. But now they are drunk.*

When they have thrown off their wine, they will repent.

Thom 28

Jesus said: It is not possible for a man to ride two horses or stretch two bows; and it is not possible for a servant to serve two masters, unless he honors the one and insults the other. No one drinks old wine and immediately desires to drink new wine. And new wine is not poured into old wineskins, lest they burst; nor is old wine poured into a new wineskin, lest it spoil. An old patch is not sewn on a new garment, for a rent would result.

Thom 47

Jesus said: He who has known the world has found the body; and he who has found the body, the world is not worthy of him.

Thom 80

It is obvious that human eyes see this world very differently from Spiritual eyes. Jesus was very clear that at no time could you combine the two. *You cannot have both worlds simultaneously.* One belongs to Man and the other to Spirit (God).

While living in this world, you must always choose between seeing with Reality/Love, or Illusion/Fear. The first is based on the infinite Moment of Now, which is another way of describing Eternity; the latter is grounded in time and space (the Human experience). At some point you may experience this Truth—but only when you are ready. As stated in Ecclesiastes, there is a time and a season for everything under the sun.

Christ Consciousness

Nearly two thousand years after Jesus introduced the mind of Christ through his example, Man still chooses to blind himself to the Truth. While there has been an evolution of consciousness, we are still locked into many of the same distorted beliefs that have been passed down from one generation to the next. It would seem that evolution can be multi-sided.

One definition of evolution says that evolution is a movement, part of a series of events that are related and sequential. From this, it can be inferred that what has worked in the past was right for that time, and at that time it was the highest Truth.

Jesus said that he was not here to tell the people that what preceded him was not true for the time it was believed. He said that he was here to bring a higher Truth. That is what evolution is. When the combined hearts and minds of mankind reach a certain point, there is a progression to a higher level. The belief systems that have served to move Man forward were necessary at the time they were in place; nevertheless, when the willingness for change is not present, the same belief systems that once served to move Man's Consciousness along his journey become the very things that hold him locked in illusion.

You cannot fully understand the word of God when you are looking through the eyes of Ego. It is only when you can see through the eyes of your Soul, and not the mind of Man, that your vision becomes clear. Not unlike any other skill, looking through the eyes of Soul takes practice. The change in vision can only be developed when you choose to see things without a judgmental mind.

Everyone has the ability to discern between Ego and Spirit. Change of vision is not obtained without effort, however. To see with different eyes you must remain constantly on guard. You must not allow your past experiences to cause you to fall into the familiar patterns of Judgment. Trusting in the unknown is not easy, and the natural thing is to rely on the intellect to determine what is Real and True. Jesus stood out in this world as teaching something very different from what Man believes.

In many ways, the words Jesus spoke could not be understood, even by the most intelligent. Throughout history, theologians and lay Christians have tried to understand their meaning. If you remember that Jesus came to change how people see, it becomes clear why so many continue to struggle with understanding. Remember, those who have tried to interpret the words were not living with the same elevated Consciousness as the man who spoke them. Few have been truly qualified to teach his message. For the most part, Man has always tried to take the Truth Jesus spoke and apply it to his Ego-based way of life. This is like trying to put a square peg into a round hole!

When you consider that in one world the energies are so slow that physical matter appears as solid, and in another the bodies are much finer and appear not to be physical, you can see that there are differences Man has not even begun to consider.

Einstein understood that his own human mind, although capable of understanding more than most, was incapable of fathoming the fullness of Creation.

My religion consists of a humble admiration of the illimitable superior spirit who reveals himself in the slight details we are able to perceive with our frail and feeble mind. The only thing that gets in the way of my learning is my education.

Albert Einstein

Many are crippled by their education, and there are many concepts that stand in the way of understanding. One such concept is the notion that Jesus was "the Only-begotten Son."

It is true that, at the time when Jesus was living as the Christ, he was in fact representative of the Consciousness of the Son. What is not true, however, is that he was the only one who comes from and is a part of the Sonship commonly known as the Son.

Every soul created by God was in fact begotten of God, and *each* contains the same attributes as Jesus; when you choose the

Consciousness of the Christ, you become one with the Christ. Remember that Christ was not Jesus' last name. Jesus became the Christ when he accepted his calling. While in the vibration of Love (non-judgment), he was cognizant of his role as the only-begotten son (the Christ Consciousness), and in those times he was and is representative of the Way, the Truth, and the Life.

> *Jesus said to him, "I am the way, and the truth, and the life; no one comes to the Father, but by me."*

Jn 14:6

When the Bible is seen as illustrating both the Fall and the return to understanding through an evolutionary process, it becomes easier to recognize the role of Jesus. The story moves through its beginning stages to the time where righteousness was taught as the goal; finally, it was recognized that this kind of thinking had to be corrected. Hence the Savior was born.

Jesus came to this world to demonstrate that it is possible for humans to overcome the limited judgmental mind of Man, and reclaim the divine essence. To accomplish this, it was necessary for him to start with the same limitations as any other human being, while embodying the higher vibration of the Sonship.

In this world, of course, most have opted for the experience of Man. This means that they experience most things dualistically, constantly at odds with themselves and others. The other option is to live in the vibration of Love/God (a unified state that exists as one). This unified state, which exists as one, is what many have come to know as the Christ Consciousness.

It is this Consciousness that Jesus ask his followers to accept, if they are willing to experience the fullness of Love and transcend the vibration of Sin. Few choose to do this, primarily because of the influence of negative energies. We have already seen that even Jesus occasionally gave in to the influence of the negative energy present in the mind of Man—when he killed a defenseless fig tree, for example. Later we shall look at the concept of Energy, and how it figures in the interplay of experience within this world.

I find it helpful to continually go back to the beginning and remember that the whole concept of Original Sin is no more than a misunderstanding. It is nothing more than identification with the human experience (the Lower Self or Ego), as opposed to living in a state of Spiritual Awareness in each moment (the Higher Self).

Sonship

Through the Crucifixion, Jesus disclosed to the world that you could only kill the body, not the Soul. This was the real meaning of his Atonement and sacrifice. By demonstrating that he was not a body, he saved Man from continuing to accept a false belief.

In spite of what has been taught by traditional Christianity, he did not take Man's sins upon himself. His teaching was that it is only one's own judgment/belief that gives sin any meaning.

This level of Consciousness is hard to accept on a day-to-day, moment-by-moment basis. Your Ego may even tell you that it is impossible; after all, you are "not like Jesus." Many have been taught that Jesus was the only-begotten Son of God. What you may not have been told, however, is that when you accept your real identity you become one with the Christ Consciousness—you become the only-begotten Son of God!

> **Sonship**
> The second person of the Trinity. The term refers to the collective group of Souls (individualized units of Consciousness).

There is a Bible passage that states, "God so loved the world that he gave his only-begotten Son" (Jn 3:16). This did not refer to Jesus as much as it did to the whole **Sonship**. By *Sonship,* I mean the Collective Consciousness, shared by all, that exists at the vibration of Spirit.

> *The God who made the world and everything in it, being Lord of heaven and earth, does not live in shrines made by man, nor is he served by human hands, as though he needed anything, since he*

himself gives to all men life and breath and everything. And he made from one every nation of men to live on all the face of the earth, having determined allotted periods and the boundaries of their habitation, that they should seek God, in the hope that they might feel after him and find him. Yet he is not far from each one of us, for 'In him we live and move and have our being'; as even some of your poets have said, 'For we are indeed his offspring.' Being then God's offspring, we ought not to think that the Deity is like gold, or silver, or stone, a representation by the art and imagination of man. The times of ignorance God overlooked, but now he commands all men everywhere to repent...

Acts 17:24-30

Repentance means allowing yourself to accept your true essence as One with God. Once this Truth is embraced and consciously called forth as an experience, you are immediately restored to a state of being where Sin (limited beliefs based on false perceptions) no longer has control over you.

If you continue in my word, you are truly my disciples, and you will know the truth, and the truth will make you free.

Jn 8:31-32

You are indeed free, once you know Truth experientially. Unfortunately, it is also true that any time you revert to a past belief you will find yourself imprisoned again, because manifested experience follows your thoughts.

I protest, brethren, by my pride in you which I have in Christ Jesus our Lord, I die every day!

1 Corinthians 15:31

Any time we revert to the judgmental mind, we are forced to view things through the filter of the human mind. Einstein understood this principle well enough to say that

A human being is part of a whole, called by us Universe, a part limited in time and space. He experiences himself, his thoughts and his feelings as something separated from the rest....a kind of optical delusion of his consciousness. This delusion is a prison for us, restricting us to our personal desires and to affection for a few persons nearest to us. Our task must be to free ourselves from this prison by widening our circle of compassion to embrace all living creatures and the whole of nature in its beauty.

It is exactly this kind of expansion beyond the human experience that leads one to the Christ Consciousness. There, you can fully share in the experience of "being in this world, and not of it." This transformation takes place when you become One with the mind of Christ.

For God has put it into their hearts to carry out his purpose by being of one mind and giving over their royal power to the beast, until the words of God shall be fulfilled.

Revelation 17:17

What is Faith?

God created a system that will respond to your every thought. The universe is impersonal, and it will give you exactly what you ask for. The universe cannot think for you. Free Will makes it impossible for the universe to change what you have asked for. You will always get what you believe you will receive. Many times, however, what your Ego is asking for and what you truly believe are two different things. This is due to the doubt that you have at the time of your request.

How do you live in this world and go beyond doubt? This is what faith is all about. Jesus often said, "Your faith has healed you." It is only after you totally surrender the will of your Ego that you are prepared to go home to God.

Evolution is the progression or unfolding of something. Everything that is free to evolve will expand eventually. Only attachments to the past stand in the way of change. If you wish to change the contents of a cup, you must empty the cup before there is room for more. One of the hardest things that Man must face is trusting in the unknown. This is why letting go of past beliefs is so difficult.

In understanding the principle and the power of belief, we are getting to the real role Jesus played in the evolution of Consciousness. Jesus came here to teach, by example, how to overcome the world and the hold that it has on those who subscribe to false beliefs. He agreed to come into this world as a man, with a mind that itself needed to be transformed from Judgment (based in Sin/Fear) to Non-judgment (based in Love).

> *"Jesus came here to teach, by example, how to overcome the world..."*

> Therefore he had to be made like his brethren in every respect, *so that he might become a merciful and faithful high priest in the service of God, to make expiation for the sins of the people.*
>
> Heb 2:17

Jesus was born with the same Original Sin (an Ego) as any other human. He did, however, undergo a profound shift. In the end, he was dramatically transformed from experiencing the limitations of a man to experiencing and symbolizing the Christ Consciousness.

> *And when Jesus was baptized, he went up immediately from the water, and behold, the heavens were opened and he saw the Spirit of God descending like a dove, and alighting on him; and*

*lo, a voice from heaven, saying, "This is my beloved
Son, with whom I am well pleased."*

Mt 3:16-17

Notice how the moment *shifted* after Jesus was baptized. If
he had been seeing with Spiritual eyes or had been born without an
Ego (a human mind), the change would not have taken place. It is
noteworthy also that, according to the story, the Lord was pleased
that he chose to accept his job, which was to show the world that it
is indeed possible to transcend the human mind.

*The Son of man came not to be served but to serve,
and to give his life as a ransom for many.*

Mt 20:28

The "life" to be laid down refers to attachment to the
personality self. The apostles showed that they knew Jesus saw
through this erroneous perception:

*And they came and said to him, "Teacher, we know
that you are true, and care for no man; for you do
not regard the position of men, but truly teach the
way of God..."*

Mk 12:14

The Christian Church

Interestingly, the Bible implies in several places that the Earth
does not move. It took men like Copernicus to deduce that the
Sun was the center of the Solar System. While there are those who
act as catalysts for change by introducing new thoughts, there are
also those who have a stake in keeping the *status quo.*

Because of this, change takes place gradually. Often those in
power, who wish to remain in control and keep the masses ignorant,
resist it. Copernicus' idea conflicted with the teaching of the Roman
Catholic Church; in order to publish it without having to fight the
Church (and lose), Copernicus modified his book to say that his
theory was only a trick to make calculation simpler. He had to state

that he was not claiming that the Earth actually moved around the Sun.

Looking back through history, we see how dangerous this kind of control is. Fear forced men like Copernicus to carefully weigh every word. Another example of this kind of control was the Church's suppression of Galileo. Galileo was convinced that he had conclusive proof for the Copernican theory, but the Church, feeling threatened, would under no circumstances allow it to be introduced. In 1633, his book was banned and he was forced to state that he had been wrong. His life was spared, but he was placed under permanent house arrest. As usual, the Church did its best to suppress change; it banned Galileo's book for almost two hundred years. It was not until 1979 that Pope John Paul II admitted that the Church had erred in its treatment of Galileo.

While Christian doctrine teaches that merely accepting Jesus as having died for your sins is enough to save you, Jesus had a different take on the matter (see Mt 7:21-23, for example). Many will find that the words Jesus spoke are in direct opposition to the dogma they have been indoctrinated with. Many of the so-called Christian churches are preaching that merely accepting that Jesus died for your sins will somehow transform you back to life. This is not true!

Jesus Spoke of What it Takes to be One of His Disciples

If any one comes to me and does not hate his own father and mother and wife and children and brothers and sisters, yes, and even his own life, he cannot be my disciple...."

Lk 14:26

That sounds like a tall order: forsake your mother, your father, your brother, your sister, even your own life. How many people, do you suppose, were willing to give up all that they had to put God first?

It is not easy to move beyond living for this world. Just as there were not many people willing to give up their lives for God 2000 years ago, there are not many people today who are willing to do it.

> *This people honors me with their lips, but their heart is far from me.*
>
> Mt 15:8

They talked of wanting God, but when faced with making the commitment required, they chose this world.

> *Watch and pray that you may not enter into temptation; the spirit indeed is willing, but the flesh is weak.*
>
> Mt 26:41

You can have good intentions and think that you desire God, but Ego is very powerful. It can overshadow your Higher Self if you are not constantly vigilant.

All souls must have the experiences necessary to choose to move beyond this world. At the time of Jesus, there were many who had not reached this state of being; two thousand years later, most are still processing, and thinking that we need to continue this process. Happily, with increased understanding comes the realization that further processing is unnecessary.

Later on, you will read that Time need not be the controller of your experiences. 2000 years ago, Jesus said that Heaven was at hand. Those who understood the principles of Time were able to skip the evolution process and take full advantage of the eternal moment of Now! Now always *is*.

Breaking the attachment to illusion is not an easy task. Jesus even spoke of driving a sword between family members. Often there is great confusion over the concept of "honoring thy mother and father" when it comes to living in Truth. "Honoring" does not mean blindly following them, or representing their human mind over their spiritual one.

> *Do not think that I have come to bring peace on earth; I have not come to bring peace, but a sword. For I have come to set a man against his father, and a daughter against her mother, and a daughter-in-law against her mother-in-law; and a man's foes will be those of his own household.*
>
> Mt 10:34-36

From this passage, you can see that Jesus was stressing the importance of each person standing firm in the Truth, regardless of the effect of that commitment on family relationships. He knew that you couldn't honor Man's idea of what is Real and still experience the fullness of Reality.

There is No Part Way Home!

> *For whoever keeps the whole law but fails in one point has become guilty of all of it.*
>
> Jas 2:10

To understand what this statement means, you must view it through Higher Self (that which sees through Spiritual, not human, eyes). It does not mean that you will be judged. It simply means that anytime you create anything from Ego, your creations will be Ego-based. You and your creations are one, and all that you create must be settled before moving on.

If you have the slightest bit of doubt or Fear and have not fully surrendered to God, you will be subject to the Karma resulting from your creations. Your commitment must be 100%.

I tell you, you will never get out till you have paid
the very last copper.

Lk 12:59

This means all debt, all Karma, must be paid before you can go home.

And this is the judgment, that the light has come
into the world, and men loved darkness rather
than light, because their deeds were evil. For every
one who does evil hates the light, and does not
come to the light, lest his deeds should be exposed.
But he who does what is true comes to the light,
that it may be clearly seen that his deeds have been
wrought in God.

Jn 3:19-21

If you feel you must hide your thoughts or actions, you can be assured you are creating for Ego in that moment, for *Fear does not exist in the vibration of Unconditional Love.* You will continue to create darkness in your life as long as you choose to live in Ego.

Free Will is Eternal

It will always remain your choice to remain in darkness; you can choose to see the light at any time, or not. One thing is certain: you will never move beyond this world as long as you are attached to it. To detach from it, you must have the Consciousness to see beyond it. This is the message of Jesus. He did not come into this world to be worshiped as God the Father and Creator of all things.

The concept that each person is in charge of his own destiny may sound too simple to be true, but even this Truth will be beyond the level of experience of most people. As explained above, the greatest obstacle to overcome is that which is most often prized as the greatest possession. I am referring, of course, to the human mind.

So great is the illusion of this world that many hold onto it as their greatest treasure. Very few individuals have developed the eyes to see; those who are holding onto this world have forsaken the infinite Self for their finite Self. Jesus stated that even the Prophets and the Righteous were still confused and limited in their ability to see True Reality:

Truly, I say to you, many prophets and righteous men longed to see what you see, and did not see it, and to hear what you hear, and did not hear it.

Mt 13:17

We shall return to why even prophets and the righteous failed at their attempt to overcome the human condition, but for now it is enough to know that it is always the human mind that causes this failure to see what is plainly in front of one's face.

While some have experienced moments of clarity and glimmers of Reality, there is only one way that true vision can be maintained. You must focus on what is outside the spectrum of normal vision, and hold on to that state of Consciousness. Failure to hold on to this treasure above all else will result in your falling back into the vibration of this world. In this world, the best that can be hoped for is to become a good Ego, interpreting things through the human mind. Although it appears that being good is better than being bad in this world, even the best Ego is far from Christ Consciousness.

There are laws of Creation that were established to regulate experiences as perceived within the mind of Man. One such law is the Law of Projection. What you project, you will experience as your perceived reality, making it impossible for you to dispel the illusion of this world. This is why it is essential to trust in the **Holy Spirit**, to intercede and translate

> **God the Holy Spirit**
> The unit of Consciousness, begotten of the Creator for the sole purpose of allowing for the experience of degrees or levels of Awareness. The bridge between the Real and the Imagined; the orchestrator of the interplay between all Dimensions within Creation.

the illusion to Reality.

Remember, your human mind can only see what it has been programmed to see. It will constantly use past programs to validate every experience as true or false. If the memory of Reality were programmed into your human mind, this methodology might work, but the fact is True Reality exists outside of the memories of the human mind. True Reality can only be experienced with the Spiritual mind. This means that you must hold to the desire for Oneness before anyone or anything.

> *The kingdom of heaven is like treasure hidden in a*
> *field, which a man found and covered up; then in*
> *his joy he goes and sells all that he has and buys*
> *that field.*

Mt 13:44

Can such a thing be done? Is it possible to forsake this world for Heaven? The answer is Yes—but very few find that they are committed enough to see it through. How about you?

> *Strive to enter by the narrow door; for many, I tell*
> *you, will seek to enter and will not be able.*

Lk 13:24

Unless you contend that the Jesus of the Gospels exaggerated the degree of commitment necessary to attain Heaven, you must admit that he says that those who are serious about their awakening cannot have any attachment to this world of illusion. This is true because one is either awake or asleep; there is nothing in between. There have been many who set out to become spiritually awakened, only to find themselves in a never-ending battle with their Egos. There even some who are so deluded by their Egos that they are not even aware they are still asleep!

The Awakening

The level of understanding necessary to see this is beyond the range of most people. Anyone who identifies with this world as the extent of his life, and honors human experience over Spiritual, in no way can accept this kind of Love. I wonder how many have ever considered what Jesus demanded of his disciples.

Many today have deluded themselves into believing that they can have both worlds; they have not accepted that this present world's attachments must be laid down. Even the original Disciples of Christ found that there were times when they could not maintain the level of detachment necessary. In the letter to Timothy, we find that Paul was feeling abandoned by Demas:

> *Do your best to come to me soon. For Demas, in love with this present world, has deserted me and gone to Thessalonica; Crescens has gone to Galatia, Titus to Dalmatia.*

2 Tim 9:10

In the Introduction to this book, I spoke of moving beyond the human mind. In fact, the only obstacle that stands between you and your understanding *is* your human mind. It is always your past belief, held on to as Truth, which creates the barrier.

> *We can't solve problems by using the same kind of thinking that we used when we created them.*

Albert Einstein

This book has been written to lead you to the Truth that will set you free, but it cannot change the direction or path you choose for your experience. Only you can do that. If you are satisfied with the world you see, and feel that you have no need to change, then do nothing and wait until you are disturbed by an inner voice.

Nevertheless, for those who wish to become free, my advice would be to begin meditating. Open yourself to hearing God/Spirit speak directly to you. At first, this method of communication may not be very clear. There may be something inside of you that is blocking the channel, and at first, you may only receive what sounds like radio static.

If this is the case, you will find it necessary to address the problem at the source. It may be advantageous to remember that Oneness is your natural state. The only thing that can block your awareness to this Truth is fixation or attachment to some aspect of the dream-state Man calls reality. Fear is the basis of all attachments to Form in this world. Fear is even at the core of what the Human mind has accepted as love—which is why Jesus said you must forsake even your own family to be his disciple.

> *Whoever does not hate father and mother as I do cannot be my disciple, and whoever does [not] love his father and mother as I do cannot be my [disciple].*

> Thom 55

Given this, it becomes obvious that you are required to discern between Man's idea of love, based on the personality's (Ego's) fears and possessiveness, and Real Love, based on the True Self (Higher Self). In order to overcome this world's hold on you, every thought must be transformed into a Higher Reality. Attachment to the worldly meaning of love—pre-existing in the mind—often is the greatest obstacle. As you move along the path of transition, you will indeed find that there are immense differences in the states of Consciousness belonging to, respectively, the mind of Man and the mind of Spirit.

Jesus said that the world in its present form is not worthy of an awakened individual.

> *Jesus said, whoever has come to know the world has discovered a carcass, of that person the world is not worthy.*

> Thom 56

To know this world means that you have moved from previous perceptions into accepting things in a totally new way.

Conclusion: The Message of Jesus Christ

My hope is that you now have a greater understanding of the mysteries of Creation. For those who have the eyes to see, it should now be clear why Jesus proclaimed:

I am the way, and the truth, and the life; no one comes to the Father, but by me.

Jn 14:6

God is and will always be Unconditional Love. To the human mind, the word "unconditional" seems to be beyond comprehension. This is why it was written that "God is Spirit" (Jn 4:24). As Spirit, you are able to comprehend that which is beyond the human experience, and experience God in the fullness of True Reality.

Jesus did not focus on the human perspective, but on his Spiritual Self. His life shows that within Man there exists something special. That something must be awakened from within; it comes forth as a rebirthing.

Jesus made the distinction between the two states of Consciousness clear when he spoke of this world and the attachment to its Form. At the beginning of his ministry, Jesus told his disciples that they were *of* this world; at the end, he said they were *no longer* of this world. The change that took place was the rebirthing within them. They no longer regarded the world as a treasure to be sought after. They knew that something far greater existed.

You, too, can have this same treasure. All that is required is that you follow the lead of your brother Jesus; you must forsake this world and all the things in it.

Man's idea of love differs greatly from that of God—so much so that Jesus called even one of his most devoted followers Satan!

But he turned and said to Peter, "Get behind me, Satan! You are a hindrance to me; for you are not on the side of God, but of men."

Mt 16:23

For those unfamiliar with the Bible, you may be surprised to discover that Peter was also the disciple whom Jesus referred to when he said, "Upon this rock I shall build my church."

How is it that in one moment Jesus saw Peter as the rock on which to build his church, and in the next identified him as Satan? The answer lies in the choice Peter was making at the time. That same choice is available to you—in that you can forsake either your human or your Spiritual life. You must choose one and deny the other.

> *"No one can serve two masters; for either he will hate the one and love the other, or he will be devoted to the one and despise the other. You cannot serve God and mammon."* Then Jesus told his disciples, *"If any man would come after me, let him deny himself and take up his cross and follow me. For whoever would save his life will lose it, and whoever loses his life for my sake will find it. For what will it profit a man, if he gains the whole world and forfeits his life? Or what shall a man give in return for his life?"*
>
> Mt 6:24-26

How many have understood this kind of commitment? How many will find their way home? Again, look to the words of Jesus; he spoke on this topic several times (see Mt 7:13-14 for example). You can easily infer that many will not find their way to Life.

There exists a great deal of confusion about Creation and Jesus' explanations of it. One of the greatest examples of this is the belief that you will be judged worthy or unworthy of Life. There is no judge to pass judgment upon you, other than the Word that was presented. Each Soul will experience the direct result of living either for God or for the Self.

There is an expression, "Ignorance of the law is no excuse." Creation works pretty much the same way. If you do not choose to

devote the time to understand and live for God, you will have to
suffer the consequences. The choice is simple: if you truly wish to
be saved and experience the fullness of God (Love)—then live each
moment for Love.

In the next section, we will look at what that means, and why
those who have never heard of Jesus may find their way to him,
even before many of the so-called Christians.

> *For, being ignorant of the righteousness that comes
> from God, and seeking to establish their own, they
> did not submit to God's righteousness.*

Rom 10:3

Part Two: You and God

In Part One, we examined the Bible and presented the teachings of Jesus Christ in the context of universal Truth. What exactly is this Truth? What is the structure of the Cosmos, and what role do we play in it?

Now we are going to deal with the "big questions" that prophets, teachers, and mystics have been trying to answer since time immemorial. God, the Soul, Time, Energy, Cause and Effect—all these concepts, and more, will be subjects of our exploration. Christ was our starting point. Now that we have better understood his message, we can try to apply it to our view of existence and our daily life.

1. God

Imagine that God is All Things

The truth is you do not have to imagine anything...because you already know it! You just don't live your life with the knowledge that you already have.

In this section, we are going to examine the Truth you already know. We will look at God, and realize he is and always has been present in every moment.

To understand God's ever-presence we must start to recognize God as *God*. There is only ONE God. Nothing exists that is not a part of God. Every truth, every lie, every belief, and every religion exists in the Consciousness of God.

Here are some attributes that have been used to describe God. They are beliefs commonly accepted by most of the major religions:

- God is *omnipresent*: he is present everywhere and at all times

- God is *omnipotent*: he is all-powerful

- God is *omniscient*: he is all-knowing, and aware of all things everywhere

Another way (and perhaps a simpler one) of expressing all this is to say that *God alone exists*. If we accept that God does indeed possess these qualities, then it follows that nothing can exist that is not a part of God.

It matters not what your belief system is or what religion you follow: if you understand these simple facts, you will see that God is *all things*, and that there is no place and no thing that is not God. Once this becomes clear, this world and the things of this world take on a new meaning. You will see all things as an opportunity for growth.

This world would certainly be a different place if this Truth were not just intellectualized, but lived as a reality. Imagine how you would feel about everyone else if you realized that not only are they like you in their humanness, they are also a part of the same Omnipresence, experiencing itself as a physical manifestation.

There are a few excerpts from the Bible that can help shed some light on this:

> *God is love, and he who abides in love abides in God, and God abides in him.*
>
> 1 Jn 4:16
>
> *There is no fear in love, but perfect love casts out fear.*
>
> 1 Jn 4:18
>
> *"For I the LORD do not change..."*
>
> Mal 3:6

Each of these verses is a powerful statement on its own; combine the three, and what you have is something absolutely essential. The natural tendency is to read the words and not fully appreciate their significance; for this reason, I would like you to take a moment and reflect on them a little longer.

God Has No Limits

God is the good as well as the bad, and everything in between. When you fully understand God, you must see that God is nothing less than everything, for God has no limits!

If you wish to expand your vision, a willingness to release all thoughts of limitation is a prerequisite. Any thought that pertains to the world of Form puts a restriction on your experiences. If you allow limitations to exist, you will become lost in the judgment of everything in your life. Where could you be holding such limited thoughts? A good starting point might be your picture of God.

How do you see God? Is your God limited? Are you open to accepting God as all things? Take a moment and ask yourself if you do recognize God as all things. Sure, you may say, yes, I do recognize God as being all things at all times…but unfortunately most people will find that they can't live with that understanding in every moment. Here is an example: picture yourself driving down the road. Suddenly, someone pulls out in front of you. What is your reaction? Do you recognize that other driver as God, and give him a smile and a wave—or do you curse him for being so inconsiderate?

> *The LORD has made everything for its purpose,*
> *even the wicked for the day of trouble.*
>
> Prov 16:4

Here you see that all of Creation was made for God, to express itself to itself. Even the wicked were created for God. Everything has a place within Creation.

This could be the most important insight you receive from this book: As long as you view things through the perception of your Ego mind, your understanding will always be limited. The limits you put on God keep you from fully understanding him.

Let's take it a step further. Picture yourself walking along peacefully. Someone attacks you without warning and robs you of all your money. Is that person God? Regardless of how you answer this question, the fact remains: *everything and everyone is God in expression.*

I think it is an understatement to say that many people will have a difficult time with this. There are so many different levels of awareness!

God is Consciousness

God is pure Consciousness. All things within Creation are merely the manifestation of God's thought and exist within his Consciousness. Everything that exists is part of God's original thought.

What is Consciousness? Consciousness is God and comes from God. Understanding Consciousness is where you begin to understand God.

Is it possible for bacteria, viruses, plants, or animals to adapt or to have a will to survive? The answer lies in Consciousness. *Consciousness is at the core of all of life and all things.* This is also true of inorganic matter, including the chair you are sitting on. If there were no Consciousness behind the laws of physics, those laws would cease to exist and there would be no order to anything in the physical worlds.

However, there is order in the physical worlds, an order that can be seen when you observe the formation of matter. Atoms, which are in constant motion, group together to form molecules. Molecules group together to form compounds. These compounds are the necessary building blocks for life and all things in the physical worlds. If you take the time to look, you will see there is order to the system, and a Consciousness that maintains this order.

All things have a place within God's Creation. All of Creation has a place within God's Consciousness. You and all things originate and exist in God's Consciousness. Therefore, it is not possible for you or anyone to be isolated or separate from God. No thought of yours could exist outside of God's Consciousness.

What you call your thoughts are, in fact, God's thoughts. You draw them to yourself through your desires.

The Mechanics of Creation

To begin to understand how this is possible, you must have a deeper understanding of God. So let us look a little closer at who or what God is. Your first clue comes from God *before* Creation.

What would it mean to be the only thing that exists? Imagine being all things, and nothing, at the same time. How could God truly know itself, if nothing else existed? The answer becomes obvious when you have a greater understanding: God could not know itself because it was the only point of reference then. There was nothing to compare itself to. Therefore, God created all of Creation to experience itself to itself.

"God alone exists."

God alone exists pretty much sums up what God is. Simply put, God is everything. Every thought exists in the Consciousness of God. In Reality, there is only one Consciousness, the Consciousness of God. This Truth is extremely difficult to accept when understood with the human mind living in Separation. In Separation, Man would rather hold the Father, the Son, and the Holy Spirit as individuals, when in fact they are all individual and united as One at the same time. This is the mystery of the Trinity.

Does God have a will? How many times have you heard when someone dies that it was "God's will?" When someone survives a plane crash and everyone else dies, many people perceive this as God's will. God has only one will, and that is for Soul and Creation to evolve. God the Father is always the observer and will never make anything happen. You and the rest of Creation, working together with the Holy Spirit, are responsible for the way in which Creation is moving.

It was written in the Old Testament and repeated by Jesus: "You are gods" (Ps 82:6; Jn 10:34). You are gods because you are creators, of sorts. By this, I mean that each of us is free to make choices that influence and change the design of things experienced.

You do create everything in your life; you always have and you always will. That is why God created you in the first place. Each Soul is part of, and is contributing to, Creation. In this world, the physical manifestations are always related to and affected by the Collective Consciousness of mankind.

So how do you contribute to Creation? How you contribute to Creation is totally up to you. Everything you do is contributing to Creation. It does not matter whether you are consciously aware of it or not. Your every thought is interconnected to the whole through an intricate thought Matrix that exists within the Holy Spirit.

Each Soul is an equal unit of Consciousness within the mind of God, just as each cell in your body is equal to all the others. No one is more or less than any other. The only difference lies in your level of Awareness. So how is it then possible for you and me and everyone to have (what appears to be) an individualized Consciousness?

God Split His Consciousness: The Mystery of the Trinity

Jesus taught us how to know the Father. He said that, if you truly want to know the Father, you must know what it means to worship him as Spirit:

> *God is spirit, and those who worship him must worship in spirit and truth.*
>
> Jn 4:24

Everything is Spirit: that which is Formless, and that which has Form. Spirit (God) was the only thing that existed before Creation, and will always be the totality of all there is. Therefore, in order to Create, God had to split, or divide its own Consciousness into parts. Without a division or split in Consciousness, no individualized aspects could exist. And because Consciousness is necessary for Creation, the illusion of Separation or individualized

Consciousness was created. This is the mysterious division of the Indivisible.

Here again, we have what appears to be a paradox. Separation is obviously impossible, because God is the totality of all things; yet without a sense of Separation there could be no individualized Consciousness, nor could there be Creation.

While it is true that all things exist in God, it is also true that, in order for God's Creation to exist, it must exist in the form of a perceived, independent state of Separate Consciousness. It must be free of control. This is why God the Father (the Creator) is the observer. By the laws of his very own Creation, he must remain the observer. Creation must be allowed to unfold and take on its own movement. If God the Father imposed his will on any part of Creation, it would lose its individualized aspect and would no longer exist.

1. *God the Son (Soul)*
   This part of the Trinity represents Soul. The Son is a conglomeration of all Souls, each with its own individualized Consciousness. Each is linked to the others, as well as to the Father and to all things within the Holy Spirit. It is Soul that truly gives God the ability to experience, because each Soul was created in the likeness of God and is capable of independently creating within Creation.

2. *God the Father/Mother (The Observer)*
   In reality, of course, God is neither masculine nor feminine. God is the totality of the Whole. This is why you (as Soul) must experience both polarities in order to become whole.

3. *God the Holy Spirit (The Keeper of Creation)*
   The Holy Spirit is a Consciousness unto itself. It houses all of Creation, both the seen and the unseen. It is the part of God's Consciousness that is home to Soul. All systems within Creation are interconnected, and exist within the

Consciousness of the Holy Spirit eternally. Indeed, all of Creation resides within the Holy Spirit, where it is forever changing and evolving.

The Trinity:
States of Consciousness

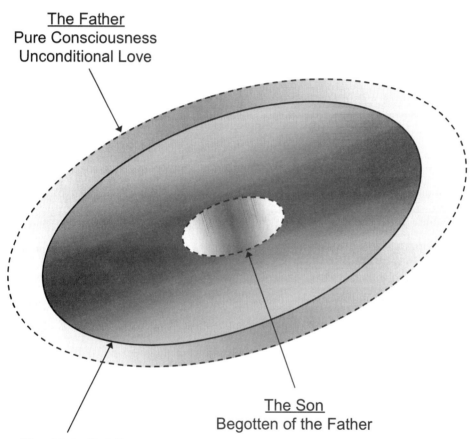

The Father
Pure Consciousness
Unconditional Love

The Holy Spirit
The bridge between
states of Consciousness

The Son
Begotten of the Father

- *The outer ring represents Unlimited Awareness*
- *The second ring is home to the Dimensions of Creation*
- *The third, inner ring represents the Consciousness of the Son (Sonship)—Pure Unconditional Love*

The Kingdom of God

Being asked by the Pharisees when the kingdom of God was coming, he answered them, "The kingdom of God is not coming with signs to be observed; nor will they say, 'Lo, here it is!' or 'There!' for behold, the kingdom of God is in the midst of you."

Lk 17:20-21

Most people have tremendous difficulty accepting that fact that the Kingdom lies within. They have always looked at this world with only the outer senses. Have you ever heard the phrase, "Looking for love in all the wrong places"?

No one can prove to you the existence of True Reality, and there are no guarantees that you will experience what I know experientially to be True. However, I can promise you one thing with complete certainty: If you do not shift your vision from your Human eyes to your Spiritual eyes, you will continue to search in vain forever.

I would like to end this chapter by repeating the most important words that you will find anywhere. They were spoken by the Father/Mother/God:

Be still, and know that I am God.

Ps 46:10

2. Time and Energy

In order to understand Time, it is necessary first to understand Energy.

Energy is the medium in which the Formless (thought) manifests itself as Form (including physical matter). Energy is present at various frequencies (rates of vibration) within all the realms of Creation. These rates correlate to the **Dimensions** referred to by Jesus when he said:

> **Dimension**
> A Plane of Creation operating within a particular frequency range of energy.

In my Father's house are many rooms; if it were not so, would I have told you that I go to prepare a place for you?

Jn 14:2

Many cannot even accept that there are worlds (Dimensions) waiting to be explored. Why? Because they cannot accept what the human eye cannot see. A major obstacle to experiencing beyond the realm of the 3D world is the senses. If something cannot be seen, felt, tasted, or smelled, most would say that it does not exist. In addition, as I stated earlier, the human mind is limited to linear experience. Here is yet another obstacle.

The concept of Time (and the reality of No Time) serve a purpose and always will co-exist within Creation. Simply put, *Time is the experience of energy within Creation that is controlled by thought*. Time is the cornerstone of Relativity.

I understand that, on the surface, the notion of Time and No Time existing simultaneously appears to be inconsistent. How can Time (movement) and No Time (non-movement) both be true at the same moment? To begin to understand this, you will have to accept that your perception of Reality is flawed—or at least a little distorted.

The more one deciphers the teachings of the Christ, the more one comprehends that within Creation there are levels of Awareness experienced by Soul. These levels exist as different Dimensions, each of which resonates at a unique frequency range; they are interconnected through an intricate Matrix. This Matrix is composed of electromagnetic energy that responds to thought. The frequency ranges correspond to the degree of Awareness of True Reality (Oneness).

Some might ask: If this is true, then why are so many blind to it? Well, although the premise is simple, actualizing the experiencing of it is another matter. In attempting to recognize this Truth, most people encounter the same problem: lack of True Vision. This is why our brother Jesus spoke so often of having "the eyes to see." In this world, confusion always derives from looking at things through the eyes of Man as opposed to the eyes of Spirit.

The eyes of Man are based on Illusion (perception stemming from Judgment), and the eyes of Spirit are based on Reality (witness to Love without Judgment). This dichotomy will remain as long as the Ego believes it is in charge of experience. Without its projecting into the future, it would cease to exist. In order to move beyond this confusion, you must constantly remind yourself that your Real or True nature is not the human mind, but something far greater and much more powerful. What I am referring to is the *Consciousness* that exists beyond Time and space.

The Paradox of Time

At the moment of Creation, God created all things. In that Eternal Moment, past, present, and future exist as one. We are now, and always will be, in that moment. *God created a perpetual system that will go on infinitely within the Eternal Moment.*

In effect, everything that exists in Creation in terms of linear Time is no more than an illusion. What makes the illusion "real" is the fact that God made his original thought of Creation eternal. This allows us to experience Time. Within Creation, there are what appear to be paradoxes. One of them is this paradox of Time.

Time is a paradox. On the one hand, there is the Eternal Moment where past, present, and future exist as one; on the other hand, there is Creation—God's eternal thought that is forever moving and evolving. It is through the movement of thought that Time exists. Without the movement of thought, there would be no Time and no Creation.

Thought is not limited to this physical Dimension. This creates many different perceptions of Time. Time to one may not be the same to another, and it is always changing relative to the observer. In addition, each Dimension operates at its own frequency or vibration, thereby affecting the way Time is perceived within it. Time in the physical worlds is much different from Time in the higher Dimensions of God. This is because the frequency of energy required to form matter is operating at extremely low rates of vibration. Time has many faces and can take on different appearances. In the physical world—where time is viewed by Ego—it is often simply a means of relating events in life.

Einstein spoke of Time as being relative to the observer. For example, in a car accident, time appears to be different for the witness as opposed to the one who is experiencing the accident. Where time seems to pass very quickly for the one witnessing the accident, it can slow down, or almost stop, for the car's occupants just before the moment of impact.

The Many Faces of Time

Time takes on many forms, and there are many variables determining what it means at any given moment. This is because Creation is multidimensional and the Consciousness of Soul is capable of experiencing different Dimensions simultaneously.

Almost everyone has had what is called a daydream. A daydream allows your Consciousness to expand beyond what you normally see while awake. In other words, you shift from consciously using your Ego mind to allowing yourself to just witness.

Understanding Time with the mind is a difficult thing to do; indeed, Man is just beginning to understand the concepts of linear time. Einstein theorized what Time meant in terms of movement in the physical worlds, and some of his theories have been proven in laboratory experiments.

One theory he proposed was that Time progresses relative to speed. In effect, if you were to take off from the earth in a rocket and could move fast enough, you could actually see yourself taking off! The principal behind the theory has been proven. A group of scientists put one atomic clock in a laboratory and took the other aboard an airplane; when they compared the time elapsed on each clock, they found there was a slight variation. The clock that was in the moving plane was behind the clock that remained motionless. From these results, they concluded that, in this world, Time is definitely affected by motion.

While Man is beginning to understand Time, he still has many misconceptions to overcome. Again, one must look beyond what the eyes can see.

When you gaze at the night sky, it would appear that what you are seeing is Real and in your present moment. Actually, what you are viewing is *not* in the present; some of the stars you are seeing no longer exist. Some burned out millions of years ago, and their light is just now reaching the Earth. In a sense, you are existing in the present and looking into the past, simultaneously!

The same can be said of everything you see. Anything that you view with your eyes requires time for the light to travel, first from the object to your eyes, and then to your brain. It is therefore impossible for the human mind to see anything in the physical worlds *in the present moment*. Every event that you witness with your eyes is already in the past. It matters not whether you are talking about fractions of seconds or millions of years; what is past is past.

The only way to experience the present is to experience it through Consciousness. This is why the mind will never allow you to live fully present in the moment. Your mind needs to think, and it needs to compare new data relative to something it already knows. Nevertheless, even with this limited tool, we are capable of seeing that Time is multifaceted.

When you move beyond using the mind, Time seems to have a different appearance. Have you ever thought about what Time means in your dreams? In your dreams, you can move forward or backward in Time. Often, the unreal seems real. As you elevate your Awareness, you may find that what you have seen as real, and what is truly Real, are two different things.

What is Matter? What is Energy?

All Creation resides within the Holy Spirit, where it is forever changing and evolving. In the physical worlds, change and the process of evolution can be easily observed. This is not only true of people and animals, but also of worlds, suns, and galaxies. At any given point there is something changing its form. There are new suns and new worlds being formed in this very moment.

Everything that takes up space in the known universe has something in common. Whether you are looking at a drop of water, a grain of sand, a cell, a rock, or a building, the common thread you find is that each is composed of matter. Matter makes the physical worlds possible.

Matter is the basic building block of all things. To understand matter in the physical realm, we must look also at energy. There could not be matter without energy. Just as Consciousness is at the core of all Life, energy is at the core of all matter.

According to Einstein's Theory of Relativity, because light has energy, it should also have mass. Because it has mass, it should respond to gravitational forces. This theory has also been shown to be true. When light from a star was observed as it passed by the Sun to reach Earth, the beam deviated from its original straight path. This happens because the Sun's huge gravitational field attracts the mass of light photons strongly enough to bend the beam. Even though the effect is infinitesimal, and it takes a body as massive as the Sun to produce it, the relationship between energy and matter is undeniable.

In modern physics, matter and energy are regarded as equivalents: they are mutually convertible. According to Einstein's formula, Energy=Mass, multiplied by the square of the velocity of Light. Using this formula, the quantity of energy in anything can be easily calculated.

Although energy is not always visible to the naked eye, today virtually everyone accepts its existence. Many experiments have shown that energy is always present in the physical world. Take a tuning fork, strike it and listen. What happens? By striking it, you are transferring your energy through the movement of your arm into the tuning fork. When struck, it starts to vibrate. Since all things are connected, the higher vibration will also affect the molecules in the air that are in close proximity to the fork.

If you touch water with a vibrating tuning fork, the molecules within the water would start to vibrate, and you would see a rippling affect on the water. This holds true, not only for the water, but also for the air. The molecules in the air alter their vibration and become a connection linking the energy to your eardrums. The vibration reaches the eardrum and is transferred through an electrical impulse to your brain.

The Law of Conservation of Energy states that the total amount of energy in the universe is constant. This means energy cannot be created or destroyed; it can only change from one form to another. The Law of Conservation of Mass Energy states that if mass is destroyed, an equivalent amount of energy must be created, so that the sum of mass energy before annihilation and the sum after annihilation are exactly equal. An example of this occurs when an electron and a positron annihilate each other: radiation is always given off, usually two or three photons are created, and their combined energy corresponds to the mass of the two original particles. Similar annihilations occur when other particles meet their antiparticles.

What does all this mean? It means that, in the physical worlds, everything exists as energy. When this energy is slowed to a sufficient rate, it can be observed as matter.

"In the physical worlds, everything exists as energy."

Today almost everyone is familiar with energy. Television, microwaves, lights, and lasers are but a few devices that use energy. We as physical beings, along with all other matter, are made up of the same energy.

This fact will lead many to a new understanding of this world. One great misperception is that there are things that are solid. Actually, nothing that exists is solid. All things in the physical realm that appear to be solid are, in fact, made up of atoms that are grouped together to form molecules. If you were to examine atoms, you would find that they are in constant motion; every one is "operating" at its own frequency.

Everything Exists at a Frequency

How things appear to you is due to their frequency or rate of vibration.

Look at water and you will see what I mean. Water appears to be a liquid, but we can change the way it appears by changing the rate at which the molecules vibrate. When we heat water to 212 degrees Fahrenheit, it starts to boil because of the transfer of energy from the source of heat. If we continue to apply heat to the water, eventually the vibration will accelerate to the point where the water will disappear! The process of evaporation means that molecules in the air have absorbed the water vapors.

The opposite effect can be observed when you reduce the rate of vibration by cooling the temperature of the water. The molecules start to move more slowly. If you continue this cooling process to a temperature of 32 degrees Fahrenheit, the molecules will move so slowly that the water takes on the appearance of being solid.

Let's recap some important points:

- Things are not always what they appear to be
- Energy exists as both positive and negative
- Like energies can combine and work together. Opposite energies tend to cancel each other out
- There is an *interconnection between all things.* Everything operates at its own frequency
- When something's frequency is changed, it takes on different properties

3. Consciousness

When I was a kid, I occasionally had philosophical discussions with my mother. We would tackle simple questions, questions that led me to examine many aspects of life. One such question was the classic, "Which came first, the chicken or the egg?"

If you were to apply "normal thinking," you would see that the chicken must come before the egg. What you experience is always rooted in thought, springing forth from deep-seated beliefs. All things follow thought through energy. In other words, first you have a thought, then you speak what you believe, then you see the result of your thought combined with the degree of belief you hold in that moment. Just as it was (and is) for God, the laws of Creation that God established are the same for all. They are totally impersonal.

The process can be summed up in three words:

Thought – Word – Manifestation

These are simple forms of energy. They are the building blocks of all of Creation. Later I will talk more on conflicting thoughts and on core beliefs. For now, it is enough to know that your thoughts are responsible, directly or indirectly, for every experience you have or will have. You can see how vitally important it is to become aware of your thoughts if you are to become free of the limitations of this world, and fulfill your real potential.

What is Consciousness?

A very important point to remember is that all Consciousness is an extension of God. In fact, every thought comes from the Consciousness of God. Nothing can exist outside the Consciousness that created it; this includes you and me, and everything seen and unseen.

Consciousness is at the core of all life and all things. What is real to you is Real because it lives in your Consciousness. You control your Consciousness. Change how you view things, and what is real to you changes.

As Consciousness is at the core of all life, let us examine our understanding of Life.

Webster's New Unabridged Dictionary defines "Life" thus: *The property of plants and animals which makes it possible for them to grow, adapt themselves to their surroundings, and reproduce their kind; it is this quality that distinguishes a living animal or plant from inorganic matter or a dead organism.*

If you look to nature, you will begin to see that God's Consciousness is at the core of all things. A will to survive is common to all life. Without Consciousness, there would be no such will. Try to kill a cockroach, for example, and you will find it has a strong desire to live; if you are not quick enough, it will find a means to escape. It recognizes you as a threat. If this were not so, it would not move when you chase it with a shoe.

Have you ever watched animals interact? Throughout the animal kingdom, you will find Consciousness. No animal could survive if it did not have Consciousness. How does a bird know to feed its young, or when it is time to push them out of the nest? Why don't migrating birds get lost when they fly south in winter? For that matter, how do they know which way is south? Some people will say this is instinct, but what is instinct? Instinct is part of the Consciousness that an animal has from birth; it helps direct the patterns of its behavior.

Look at any plant and you will see that it, too, has a desire to live and will adapt the best it can to its surroundings. Move a plant from one location to another, and it will start to lean toward the Sun. Move it again, changing its facing away from sunlight, and it will try to adjust to the new location. What does this mean? It means that all of life has some form of Consciousness within it or controlling it.

God is omnipresent and lives in all things

Because Man feels he is the most evolved form of life on this planet, he forgets that God is omnipresent and lives in all life and all things. Consciousness can be seen in all forms of life. God is expressing himself in everything that exists.

Quite simply, the body is a machine that carries you around. You are Consciousness in a physical body. You may be unaware that your Consciousness controls your body and its functions. What about when you are sleeping? Who is in control then? You are so much more than the image that you have or have allowed others to give you. Is an outside force controlling you, or are you in control?

The truth is that you, through choices, influence every experience you have in your life. Just as it takes your Consciousness to move your toe or your ankle, it takes your Consciousness to alter events or circumstances in your life.

The statement that "We are made in the image of God" is true. God is the totality of all things, just as you are the total of the parts of your Consciousness. You are an individualized aspect of

God. You have a Consciousness unto yourself, yet you will always have a link to God, and God will always have a link to you.

The Whole Mind—Your Link to All of Creation

The mind is a tool that Soul uses to interact with Spirit, in order to alter or effect changes in experiences. It is the blend of higher and lower minds. It is like a computer, because it stores data and retrieves it when needed. It is a device that communicates with the Collective Consciousness of this world and the worlds beyond.

Your mind will always do what it is programmed to do. Once programmed, it will continue to run in that program until you change it through the input of new data. If you want to change something, you must picture it as though it already existed. Why? Because the mind can only feed back what it has been given.

For example, let's say you are a smoker and are trying to quit. You must be able to see yourself as a nonsmoker, or you will be telling your mind that you are a smoker trying to quit—and you will therefore suffer all the usual painful "withdrawal" symptoms. If your mind sees you trying to do something in struggle, struggle is what you will experience.

The mind does not have a personality; it is a reactive tool. In every situation, your mind will *react* rather than *think* for you. It is up to you to do your own thinking and control the thoughts you have. These thoughts will come from either your Ego or your Higher Self— the source will be determined by the choice made by the I Am of your soul.

> *For from within, out of the heart of man, come evil thoughts, fornication, theft, murder, adultery...*
> Mk 7:21

"From within" refers to Consciousness, not the mind; the mind is not capable of independent thought.

Ego

Ego is an aspect of your Consciousness, and is capable of influencing many things. If you allow Ego to run your life, it will continuously create false images that appear real in your mind. It is up to you to maintain control over your thoughts and your Ego. Initially, you will need to have faith enough to trust in God.

> *And when they bring you to trial and deliver you up, do not be anxious beforehand what you are to say; but say whatever is given you in that hour, for it is not you who speak, but the Holy Spirit.*
>
> Mk 13:11

When you choose your God Self over Ego, you become a receiver or a channel, not a thinker. It is no longer necessary for you to plan and know the outcome of every situation. You become awakened to your oneness with God, and are content to live in the present moment.

> *And you will know the truth, and the truth will make you free.*
>
> Jn 8:32

True freedom comes when you allow God or Spirit to run things in your life. You are turning over all responsibility or Karma you would have created for yourself. While in Ego, you are responsible for all your creations, and your creations are directly related to your thoughts. You alone are the one that controls your thoughts.

Many people are unaware of the fact that they control their every thought. This is because they have given up control to their Egos. Ego maintains control by keeping them believing that everything is outside of them and beyond their control. In a sense, while living in Ego you are asleep to your core Consciousness, the *I Am* of your Soul.

Reprogramming

If you don't take the time to continually see God as all things, your Ego will pull you back into old habits. You will not be able to maintain your highest Truth. There is a razor's edge between seeing with the eyes of Soul and with the eyes of Man. In order to change how you view things, you have to reprogram your mind to accept a Higher Truth.

It *is* possible to reprogram your mind to always do the bidding of your God Self. But it has to be your desire. "Reprogram" is the key word here. Since the mind is a reactive tool, if you are not consistent with the imaging you put into it, your mind will not know what you want. When you realize that you are a self-creator, you will understand the importance of being consistent with your thoughts.

This is often extremely difficult, because your mind has been programmed in a variety of ways. Just as a computer uses different programs to do different jobs, the mind uses different programs in different situations. You are not the same person to your mother that you are to your best friend. You are not the same person to an acquaintance that you are to a boss at work. Which one is the real you?

The truth is that they *all* are you. You have programmed yourself (via conditioning) to adapt to the circumstances in your life. Like a computer, your mind will always play the program that you ask for. To ask for a specific program, you must be Conscious—or your Ego will decide what program to run. Most times, you will find that you are reacting rather than interacting. Your mind tends to follow the path of least resistance and play the most familiar tape. If you are not clear on what it is that you want, how will your mind play the tape or program necessary to bring about change?

When you decide that you want to change something in your life, you have many possible programs that your mind can feed back to you. Will you summon the old programs you have long identified with, or the new ones that you are beginning to create? Which one do you think your mind is going to choose for you? If you do not have a strong, conscious desire for your new program, your mind will play the one most familiar. Change happens over a period of time. You must reset each program, one at a time. Just when you think that you have addressed every one and have evolved to a New You, an old trigger pops up—and Ego calls for an old program to play again. This frequently initiates a process that leads you back into living for Ego and what is comfortable and familiar.

Old programs are groups of thoughts that are stored away. They are just waiting to be brought back to the forefront of your Consciousness. Your mind may either take a familiar path or be directed Consciously. The process of elevating your Consciousness and gaining control of your Ego is, at first, frustrating; it requires you to be conscious of Self, and Ego has developed most of the programs you have stored away.

The way in which the mind works is analogous to electricity. Both always follow the path of least resistance. You must create the resistance to the old pathways, or the old, familiar way will win out every time.

Your Mind as Receiver and Transmitter

Your mind is a receiver and transmitter; it sends and receives thoughts. In order to become a channel for Spirit, you must exercise control over your Ego and quiet the Ego mind. Quieting the Ego mind requires you to maintain control over reactive thoughts based in past memories and erroneous beliefs.

Every thought that you have is based on your level of Awareness in that moment. In the broadest sense, what you create within your Consciousness becomes part of Creation. Every thought creates movement at some level. *It is through the movement of thought that Creation moves.* It does not matter if you are in one Dimension or another; the principles are the same. The only difference is the speed at which your creations manifest themselves.

The physical worlds are very slow and dense. While in the physical, your creations take time to manifest themselves. God intended this way for the world. It gives you the time to view your creations before they are complete. Upon reflection, you will see that not every thought makes it into Form, and more likely than not, the things that have been created are different from your originating thoughts. This is caused by the Matrix of energies constantly changing, adjusting, and interconnecting with the rest of Creation.

The Matrix of Creation

When Jesus spoke of "Worlds upon Worlds," he was referring to the many different levels of Consciousness that exist within the Matrix of Creation.

The Matrix is the infrastructure of Creation. Within the Matrix lie all the different levels or Dimensions that appear to be separate, yet are interconnected to form Creation. While in the truest sense, there is no Separation in God and all things are one, there do exist parts within the whole. There is a core where all the energy that fuels Creation originates. The core is the point where the frequency is at its highest. It is also the point of origin of Soul. As you move away from the origin, the rate of vibration slows the particles of energy. Eventually, they slow to the point where they can be viewed as matter.

Within the Matrix, all thoughts are connected and interconnected. Each thought attracts other thoughts vibrating at a similar rate or frequency. These groups spiral outward in waves, until they reach the outer edges of Creation; there, they start their return trip back to the source.

The rate of vibration correlates to its place within the spiral. The frequency is highest at the core, and slows as it reaches the outer rings. Within the spiral are what have been referred to as levels, plateaus, or Dimensions. Each level governs a specific range of unique frequencies. This is analogous to broadcast radio stations: each station uses electromagnetic waves to carry its signals. What sets one station apart from the others is the frequency of its signals.

Within the One Thought of Creation, there is movement by thought. Each Soul is partially responsible for that movement. Just as Creation itself began as a Thought in the Consciousness of God, all your creations begin as thoughts within your Consciousness. All of Creation is interconnected by thought.

Within the Matrix, there are pathways to link thoughts. Each pathway is associated with a certain frequency. These different thought frequencies allow for the existence of different Dimensions.

Although the mind is incapable of seeing the entire Matrix of thought within Creation, you can get a general idea of how it works from viewing your own body. Your body is a network of cells that are interconnected. To move any part of your body, you first have the thought to move it, and then the thought follows a certain pathway to achieve the desired result.

Movement within the Matrix of Creation works in the same way. First, you have an original thought that starts down a pathway to link with other thoughts vibrating at the same or a similar frequency. The Consciousness of the Holy Spirit then considers all the variables, and blends the vibrations from your thoughts with the vibration of all the other thoughts within Creation. Something new has been created in that moment!

You are Consciousness within the Consciousness of God.

Planes of Existence
Dimensions of Time and Space

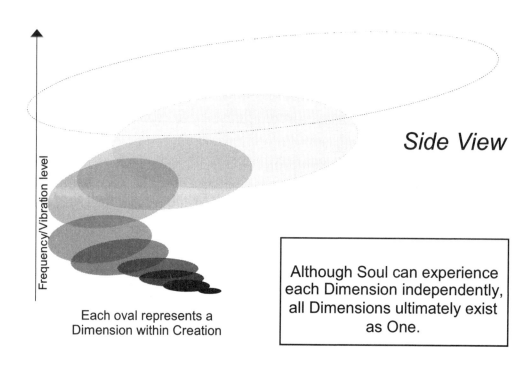

Side View

Frequency/Vibration level

Each oval represents a
Dimension within Creation

Although Soul can experience
each Dimension independently,
all Dimensions ultimately exist
as One.

Key

- Physical Worlds; re-
  stricted by linear
  Time

- Spiritual Realms;
  higher frequencies

- God; All That Is; the
  Summation of the
  Whole

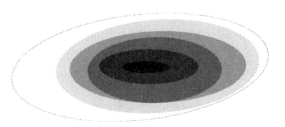

Top View

4. Spiritual v. Material

One view is limited and incomplete, while the other is unlimited, whole, and complete. Which is which?

If you accept the limited view, unlimited Awareness will remain obscure. One important metaphor found in the Bible compares Awareness to light. The light signifies seeing Reality; the dark refers to illusion. If you wish to know the whole, you must look beyond the parts—if you are too busy looking at the trees you will never see the forest. To truly know God, you must not look at particular aspects. You must see the whole.

The Bible describes God as Love, and then adds other adjectives to complete the picture. Taken individually, each adjective would leave you with an incomplete picture. To reach beyond normal comprehension, it is necessary to blend the elements and accept them as integral parts of one whole. For example, it is clear that the word "Love," as used in the Bible, has a different connotation from the everyday term. To understand it fully, it is necessary for you to move beyond your human mind.

According to The Course in Miracles, in every given moment you are experiencing either that which is Real or that which is Illusion. This keeps it simple. In any moment, you are experiencing either Love or Fear, with Love being Real and Fear being illusory. Although a fearful experience is not Real in terms of True Reality, this does not mean that you cannot experience Fear as *your* reality.

This kind of experience leads to a feeling of Separation. Many people hold to the notion that they are separate from God. In fact, many of the dogmatic teachings of religion have led men to believe that Separation is a Reality within Creation. This belief—existing in the mind of Man or in the separated Self—must one day be confronted and overcome in order to experience the whole (God, Love, Light, Reality).

Jesus said: This heaven will pass away, and the one above it will pass away; and those who are dead are not alive, and those who are living will not die. In the days when you ate of what is dead, you made of it what is living. When you come to be light, what will you do? On the day when you were one, you became two. But when you have become two, what will you do?

Thom 11

Let us see if this can shed some light on the situation. Jesus is saying here that there are various steps or Dimensions that are contained within Creation, and that they are available for experience. He is speaking metaphorically, referring to one's own experience and not to the disappearance of these heavenly realms. When he states that the dead are not alive, he means that anyone who does not recognize the Real (God, Love, Light) is not truly alive.

The last two lines may appear confusing at first glance, but after reading the Genesis account of the Fall from Grace, they should become clear. *One* refers to the state of Consciousness that existed before the perception of Separation came into the mind of Man. That God alone exists (the Oneness) is something every Soul begins with and experiences as Real. *Two* represents the split. The parts resulting from this split are sometimes referred to as a Higher Self and Lower Self. It is important to remember that this split could only happen after accepting a belief in Duality (right and wrong); the Tree of Knowledge of Good and Evil in Genesis exemplified this.

Essentially, Jesus is asking: What will you do when you become aware that you are not whole within your Self, when you realize that there is a part of you that is greater and more aware than your Ego mind?

There is a monumental difference between states of Consciousness, and between the experiences available in these different states. Once again, we find that Einstein had a great deal of insight in this regard:

A human being is a part of the whole called by us The Universe, a part limited in time and space. He experiences himself, his thoughts and feelings as something separated from the rest...a kind of optical delusion of his consciousness. *This delusion is a kind of prison for us, restricting us to our personal desires and affection for a few persons nearest to us.* Our task must be to free ourselves from this prison *by widening our circle of compassion to embrace all living creatures and the whole of nature in its beauty.*

If you realize this Truth, you must decide which part of Self will rule over each moment of experience. This is what Jesus was alluding to when he asked, in effect, What will you do when the personality wakes up from the deep sleep known to Man as the real world?

> **"What will you do when the personality wakes up from the deep sleep known to Man as the real world?"**

If you are to be successful in moving beyond the Lower Self (the prison), all limiting beliefs must be replaced with more expansive ones. It is helpful to remember that what the mind sees and believes is always setting the stage for your experience. Experience always follows thought. Later I shall go into more detail as to why it seems that you are not the originating cause of all your experiences, but for now let me assure you that everything you experience is connected to your vibration (frequency), which is in turn determined by your thoughts and core beliefs. You cannot help but experience what you put your strongest belief in. Everything in Creation moves by the power of thought.

Gandhi understood this enough to declare:

You must be the change you wish to see in the world.

As Eternity is beyond the movement of thought, time, or space, it can only be experienced. (Although I am using the word "experience" here, this word is not quite appropriate; as Man understands it, an experience must be compared to something from the past, and within the vibration of the Now there is no past. Everything simply *is*.)

Only your *Spiritual Eyes* are capable of communicating beyond the limits of Time and Space. For Man, these eyes are a very specialized medium that must be developed. The Gospel of Thomas states:

> *Jesus saw some infants who were being suckled. He said to his disciples: These infants being suckled are like those who enter the kingdom. They said to him: If we then become children, shall we enter the kingdom? Jesus said to them: When you make the two one, and when you make the inside as the outside, and the outside as the inside, and the upper as the lower, and when you make the male and the female into a single one, so that the male is not male and the female not female, and when you make eyes in place of an eye, and a hand in place of a hand, and a foot in place of a foot, an image in place of an image, then shall you enter [the kingdom].*

> Thom 22

The "eyes" Jesus was referring to are part of the transformation or metamorphosis that you go through as you shift your focus away from this world. Although the eyes see everything in a different light, it is your mind that must change: it must allow the shift to begin. Only then will your vision become unblocked.

Once this vision is activated, you begin seeing and recognizing the infinite presence of God in both the seen and the unseen worlds. It will be repeated many times in this book that *you and you alone* must determine the extent of your experiences. Each choice you make will affect the degree of expansion (or contraction) of your vision.

The physical, which exists in the Consciousness of God, is but one Plane of Existence within the system created for the evolvement of Soul. Many people identify themselves with this physical life, and believe they were born with the birth of their bodies. The truth is, you were begotten as Soul and will always be Soul, no matter where your awareness happens to be at any time.

No one has ascended into heaven but he who descended from heaven, the Son of man.
                                                    Jn 3:13

Soul existed before it came into the physical worlds, and it will continue on its journey when it leaves them. The physical worlds can be a short period in the unfolding of Soul's Higher Self; alternatively, Soul can choose incorrectly and remain in the physical worlds for all of Eternity. The Law of Free Will guarantees that you will always be the one to decide. Nevertheless, the Law of Free Will is not independent of other laws within Creation, such as the Law of Cause and Effect.

Keeping this in mind, it can be seen that life truly is an opportunity to unfold your Awareness and move ahead on your journey home. It can also be an opportunity to suffer the consequences of wrong choices.

All experiences are rooted in your Consciousness. Every event in your life originated from a thought that you have had. As long as the original thought exists, your reality will in some way reflect that thought. Change the thought, and either your life will change or it will adjust to your new perception!

Evolution

Evolution is a process of unfolding that is composed of a series of movements. Evolution is not different from any other movement. It requires Energy to fuel it. The vibration of Energy present regulates the movement. This Energy is always fluctuating and is directly linked to the Genuine Will of the collective. That is why there are so many plateaus, peaks and valleys associated with the evolution process. Once at a level or plateau, there is no movement if the Energy present stays within a certain range of vibration. When the collective thought becomes a majority, there will be a progression or regression, depending on the vibration of that Energy.

Evolution is part of Creation, and will always be part of it. Whether you are looking at Soul, this world, the universe, or Creation, you are observing evolution. This is why you must look at its physical, mental, and the spiritual aspects. Each is taking place simultaneously—but not necessarily at the same pace. There is a difference in the respective rates of movement only because Man or Soul has been given Free Will to create whatever he desires. The percentage of Love-based thought as opposed to Fear-based thought engenders vibrations unique to each moment. Wherever the Energy is directed, you will see movement.

History demonstrates the process of physical evolution. It has been well-studied and documented. Almost everyone today is familiar with the development of life, from one-celled organisms to simple forms of life and on to the more advanced mammals. This process began at the time Earth was formed. The original material for life was composed of water, hydrogen, methane, and ammonia. Later, as the planet developed an atmosphere, there were more advanced organic compounds formed, including amino acids, the basic building blocks of life. Along the path of evolution, all forms of life have undergone many changes.

Just like the patterns of physical evolution in this world, there are changes in the development of thought. Man's Consciousness develops to a certain point, and then maintains that level for a period. Man started in a primitive state with primitive tools. Little by little, he developed his brain, passing on what he had learned from one generation to the next. Many life forms have had to adapt in order to survive; some have become extinct due to their inability to change. It is no different for Man.

Change does not come easily. When change becomes too much of a threat, resistance intensifies. Throughout history, there are examples of both forward and backward movement. There have been great periods of learning and growth, followed by periods of stagnation or even regression. Again, if you look to the past, you will find that many times, it was Man's resistance to change that was the cause of the destruction of great civilizations.

The strongest resistance to change often occurs just before a major movement. It is the nature of the Ego to find a place of comfort, and want to stay there. How much forward movement do you think can take place when the collective Energy is complacent? What is the significance for all of Creation when one man has the willingness to stand alone in his Truth, no matter what the consequences are?

Where would the world be if there were no men like Columbus? His contemporaries believed the world was flat, but he was convinced that it was round. Where would the world be without unconventional thinkers? All too often, it is not until after the movement has already taken place that the majority can accept change.

One might think that Man's Spirituality would develop at the same rate as his Ego mind, but this is not so. You have Free Will. Man creates his own reality, both individually and collectively. You can easily observe the great strides forward in the history of Man's intellect. Technology is moving at an incredible rate. Computers are prime examples: what was "state of the art" only six months ago is almost obsolete today. Man has walked on the Moon and journeyed under the sea. Today there are all kinds of weapons developed for mass destruction. At any time, we could destroy ourselves. Keeping in mind the general state of the world today, is it not obvious that our Spiritual awareness has not kept pace with our Ego creations?

Each Soul is on its own path. One breaks away from a group, another follows, and then another...until you have a majority.

Eventually, you form a new group Consciousness. Then the process repeats itself. The amount of Energy that each Soul is capable of contributing is directly related to its level of Consciousness. This is the process of Evolution. Your willingness to accept change will determine how much you resist your own evolution.

You are More than This Physical Body

In order to reach Atonement (*at-one*-ment) Consciousness, you must become totally detached from this world. This is an extremely difficult thing to do. It is easy to forget what you came here for; you can easily take on a kind of amnesia. Not only may you fail to address your spiritual mission in this lifetime, you may also create new Karma—Karma that can move you, in this life, further away from your goal.

You, as Soul, are here for a purpose. Your ultimate goal is to become a conscious co-creator with God (as opposed to a Self-creator), and to elevate your Consciousness beyond that of this world. God the Father will never judge you or interfere with your creations. You have Free Will. The degree of your Soul's unfolding is in your hands. You are free to *be*, if you so choose.

Take your body, for example. As noted earlier, the way your body functions is representative of the way Creation works. The human body is a universe unto itself. But Man does not take the time to see it for what it is. God used the same basic blueprints, so to speak, for all things in Creation. Once you have a fundamental understanding of one system, you can apply that understanding to another.

> *"Your ultimate goal is to become a Conscious co-Creator with God, and to elevate your Consciousness beyond that of this world."*

In the known universe, everything that exists is composed of particles that can be broken down further, until you end up with one basic subatomic particle. What does this tell us? God created a physical dimension, starting with the smallest and simplest structure. He then continued to build upon it, using the same basic pattern to make more evolved structures.

God created your journey in the same way. You start with little or no understanding; by means of your experiences, you start to remember; this elevates your vibrations and moves you to a higher level of understanding. You are Consciousness, and Consciousness is not the body. The body is merely a vehicle to shield and move your Consciousness within this physical world.

Whether you are in the middle of a city, constantly interacting with people, or living as a hermit deep in the woods, your existence will have some kind of impact on the rest of the human race. This is what is meant by the statement that Life is Dualistic. Even though you are an individualized Consciousness, it is illusory to think that you are separate from the rest of God's Creation.

Illusion

All of Creation, as viewed within the dream state that Man has adopted as the real world, is an illusion. In the fullness of Reality, anything that you can think of existed first in God's Consciousness. When Soul chooses to create anything, it draws upon the universal mind of God. The Holy Spirit is the mind of God, so to speak. Soul is not capable of creating anything outside of God's Consciousness. *God alone exists*, and all thought belongs to God.

Nothing is actually *Real* in the sense that we normally perceive it. All things exist in the Now, including the past, present, and future; this is the true meaning of the Eternal Moment. While asleep to the Now Moment, Man's reality is similar to a dream. Just as you create in a dream that which *seems* real, what you create in the physical world seems real in that moment. The difference between experiences in various realms has to do with levels of Awareness.

Everything within Creation is either an experience based on Reality or a real experience within the dream state. In the dream state, you are creating what you think is Real but, in the truest sense, it is no different from your dreams when your body is asleep. In the physical world, you are part of a collective dream. You will remain there until you remove yourself.

How? By elevating your Consciousness beyond this physical world, by unplugging your Consciousness from the collective. You can be either a part of the illusion or an observer, seeing it for what it is.

> *Jesus answered, "My kingship is not of this world..."*
>
> Jn 18:36

As you elevate your Consciousness, you will move through your creations with greater Awareness. Your perceptions will continue to change. This is the process that all Souls go through. It is a process of unfolding. When most people speak of this world, they have a very distorted idea of its relationship to the whole of Creation. They have to expand their view in order to see the larger picture.

This larger picture is inclusive of other worlds (realms). Jesus demonstrated this to Peter and James when he met with Moses and Elijah (the Transfiguration; Mt 17:3), prophets who had been dead for centuries, "and behold, there appeared to them Moses and Elijah, talking with him."

When you elevate your Consciousness enough to become the Observer, you will recognize this world as the summation of all Souls acting collectively to form the Consciousness of this planet. All things exist in God's Consciousness as infinite potential experiences. In every moment, there are infinite possibilities for Creation! When you create, you are attracting thoughts to yourself and seeing them as your own. In a sense, they are yours; in another sense they are not, because all thought belongs to God.

What you want to accept as real within the dream state is experienced as real only as long as you make it real. How do you view it? That is what makes it real to you. When you change your perception, it takes on a new meaning.

So where is Reality, and where is Illusion? As your perception changes, your reality changes with it. What seems real to you in one moment becomes an illusion in the next, as you move in Consciousness.

The greatest illusion of this physical life occurs when you limit your awareness to the things of this world. You are part of the whole of Creation. You always have the choice: to accept that or to separate yourself from it.

In the Beginning...was *God*

Here we have the first problem Man faces in understanding Creation. In terms of the *human* mind, it is impossible to fathom. When I speak of the human mind I am referring to the brain, the storage center that contains past memories relative only to this life; I am not referring to the *Higher* Mind—your real essence and your link to All That Is. The human mind (unlike God) understands things only linearly: the present is linked to the past, which sets the stage for the future. This type of thinking is the basis for all perceptual experience in this world (usually referred to as the 3D or the three-dimensional world).

As long as you limit your awareness to this Dimension and have an attachment to its Form, you will be forever blinded to the greater Reality. What you are doing in this case is limiting your awareness to perception only. It is like looking at a shadow and thinking that the shadow image is real; the image exists all right, but you will see that there is something more if you change your line of vision.

Whenever one holds too tightly to the five senses, one is isolated from the rest of Creation. By *isolated* I mean separated in terms of experience only; in fact, there can never be a time when you are truly separated from the rest of All That Is (God).

The most important point here is that *you* put limits on the extent of what you can experience. As hard as this may be to accept at this point, there is nothing outside of the Self that can dictate how much of the whole you may be aware of. If your vision is limited to the world around you, it is because you have chosen to maintain this limitation. Einstein put it this way:

> *A human being is part of the whole called by us universe, a part limited in time and space. We experience ourselves, our thoughts and feelings as something separate from the rest. A kind of optical delusion of consciousness. This delusion is a kind of prison for us, restricting us to our personal desires and to affection for a few persons nearest to us. Our task must be to free ourselves from the prison by widening our circle of compassion to embrace all living creatures and the whole of nature in its beauty... We shall require a substantially new manner of thinking if mankind is to survive.*

As long as you maintain the same beliefs, you will see the same illusions. Einstein understood this, and encouraged people to correct their thinking:

> *A problem cannot be solved with the same mind that created it.*

If you refuse to allow yourself to see things differently, you will always see them the same way. For years, scientists have asserted that we use only 10% of our brain, the rest lying dormant. Imagine for a moment if you were to access even another 10% of your brain. What could be discovered? What are the possibilities? I am sure the answers would indeed surprise us.

Unfortunately, most people are perfectly content to remain restricted to what they have been taught are their limits. The vast majority of people in this world never realize their full potential, because they follow not their own but someone else's beliefs.

Christ explained very well the consequences of such behavior:

> *Let them alone; they are blind guides. And if a blind man leads a blind man, both will fall into a pit.*
>
> Mt 15:14

Many people in this world continue to follow "blind guides," and they have tremendous difficulty accepting the fact that the Kingdom lies within them. They have always looked at this world with only the outer senses.

No one can prove to you the existence of True Reality, and there are no guarantees that you will experience what I know experientially to be there. But I can promise you one thing with complete certainty: If you do not shift your vision from your Human eyes to your Spiritual eyes, you will continue to search in vain forever.

5. The Soul

The Anatomy of Soul

Unlike physical birth, every Soul is born identical and equal to every other. God does not play favorites!

In the moment of Creation, Soul is pure Consciousness. Begotten of God, the Consciousness of All That Is, each Soul has within its core the same memory of that Consciousness. Just as at the moment of physical conception there exists a genetic code necessary for trillions of cells yet to be formed, Soul, at its Creation, contains the Consciousness of all things.

Despite this, Soul is blinded to the Truth that it already knows. Why? So it can have a purpose; so it can experience and create. Like a man with amnesia, Soul's memory is not erased. It is merely hidden from Consciousness. This is the only way that each Soul can experience its own journey. In addition, each Soul's journey is similar: it goes from the Light (pure knowledge) to the Dark (blind to Truth), and back to the Light.

The Soul is one Consciousness, but it exists as separate parts so that you can exercise Free Will. This choice, so essential to Creation, is made possible only through a division in your Soul. Whether you evolve past this world or not, the basic components that make up your Soul do not change. For Soul was created to have three parts, and it is vitally important to know them:

1. *I Am*
2. *Ego*
3. *Higher Self*

The Anatomy of Soul

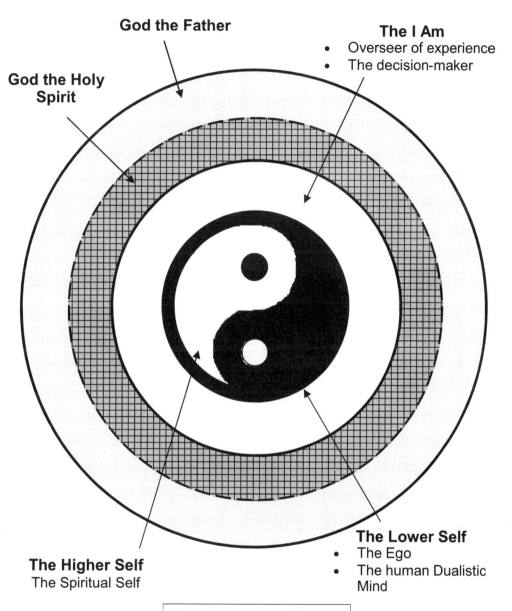

God the Father

The I Am
- Overseer of experience
- The decision-maker

God the Holy Spirit

The Higher Self
The Spiritual Self

The Lower Self
- The Ego
- The human Dualistic Mind

The structure of Soul is similar to the structure of Creation

I Am Who I Am

Each person has what some call the *I Am* of the Soul. The I Am is at the core of who and what you are. Without it, you would be nothing, and you would not be capable of Self-Awareness.

The I Am is the summation of the whole Soul. Just as God the Father is the totality of the Godhead, the I Am is the totality of its parts. At the birth of Soul, the I Am is pure Consciousness. Within the core Consciousness of the I Am, there is a desire to return home to God.

But there is a built-in problem. Ego is present, trying to create a permanent home in this world. In order for each Soul to play its role in Creation, it must have the ability to choose one thing over another (Free Will). As mentioned earlier, the Consciousness or perfect knowledge of your I Am is obscured beneath many layers or veils (amnesia). Hence the birth of your Ego.

The actual director of the energy you set into motion is the I Am part of your Consciousness. The I Am is the totality of this lifetime, as well as all the others. The I Am is the true decision-maker. The I Am is the core Consciousness, deciding in every moment to empower either the Ego or the Higher Self. In this world, many have mistakenly adopted the Ego as their True Self. These people have consciously separated themselves from True Reality.

It doesn't matter which aspect of the Soul is seemingly being given the control; ultimately the Ego and the Higher Self are merely servants to the I Am.

Whether you are aware of it or not, the goal of every Soul, according to God's will, is to awaken itself and stay enlightened.

Therefore it is said, "Awake, O sleeper, and arise from the dead, and Christ shall give you light."
Eph 5:14

Regardless of the path each Soul is on, there is a process to reach this state of Awareness. In this world, the only way the I Am of your Soul can maintain control over Ego is by remaining awake! Only then can it consciously choose to empower the Higher Self, and become a co-creator with God.

The process that moves you to this state of Consciousness happens over time. It is directly related to the desire of the I Am to choose to live for God by choosing the Higher Self over the Ego. Here again, you can see that it comes down to *choice*. It is not a certainty that your Soul will continue on the path to Enlightenment; that would violate God's most basic law, the Law of Free Will.

Free will is not a temporary thing that God gives to you. At some point in time, God does not say, "Okay, you have played long enough, it's time to come home!" Free will is eternal. You can choose to remain lost in Ego for eternity; or you can, in this very moment, make a conscious choice to live for God (Love).

To see this Truth, you have only to open your eyes and look at the world around you. Mankind is still living in hatred and indifference. When you remember that nothing can exist that is not already a part of God, you will see that Man's hatred is actually his indifference to Love (God). This is the result of the belief in Fear (*False Evidence Appearing Real*).

The Ego = Easing God Out

What does it mean to ease God out? It means to allow no room within your mind. In this world, Ego appears to be a Consciousness unto itself. It is that part of Soul designed to keep you from remembering your True Essence (being one with God/Love). It is Ego's function to keep you so busy living in its creations that you cannot see past them. Although Ego appears to be negative in most cases, actually it is neither negative nor positive. It is a necessary part of the Soul and, without it, Soul could not experience the fullness of creation.

Don't think that choosing your Ego over your Higher Self will not have bad consequences. Paul said, "Everything is lawful for me, but not all things are helpful" (1 Cor 6:12).

Once control is given over to it, Ego will continue to run on past programming, seemingly creating on its own until the I Am exercises its authority. Ego wants to create the illusion that the things of this world are important; it wants to keep you in fear of losing those things. In fact, Fear is Ego's greatest tool. It is quite good at using the things of this world to manipulate you and your thinking.

> *"Fear is Ego's greatest tool."*

The only way to overcome the Fear created by Ego is through detachment from the things that are feared—and the only way you can become detached is through the Unconditional Love of God. We release our fears when we release our desires for the things of this world. When describing the cause and result of Man's fears, the Buddha said it best: "Desire is the root of all suffering." Desire nothing but Love (God), and you cannot experience suffering. By having attachments in this world, you allow Ego to continue to have control over you.

When I am talking about attachments, I am not only referring to material things. I am referring to anything and anyone that you do not relate to with Unconditional, Divine Love. Ego-based love will restrain you from the higher vibrations needed to transcend this world. This is why Jesus stressed so heavily the need to forsake everyone and everything in this world that is not being held in the vibration of Unconditional (perfect) Love. Unconditional Love is the only way to eliminate all Fear.

> *There is no fear in love, but* perfect love casts out fear. *For fear has to do with punishment, and he who fears is not perfected in love.*
>
> 1 Jn 4:18

Many do not understand Perfect Love well enough to let go of their fears; on the contrary, they have grown to accept them as the way of life here in this world.

In the early stages of its evolution, the I Am is largely blind. This allows Ego to have pretty much a free rein over your creations. When Ego is the controlling force behind Soul, your creations will be self-serving. Perhaps now you can better understand how horrible things can happen in this world!

Ego is just as much a part of your Soul as the Higher Self. The Ego makes it possible for you to believe in the illusion of Separation. As long as you live in Ego thoughts, your Soul will remain at least partially blind to God. If you choose to live for God, you will find that Ego does not relinquish control easily. This world is a world created for Ego.

Onward and Upward: The Higher Self

The third part of Soul is your Higher Self. It is the exact opposite of Ego. While Ego is concerned only with the things of this world and operates from the vibration of Fear (Separation), the Higher Self is concerned with serving God. It operates from the vibration of Love (Oneness). When you empower your Higher Self, you become a co-creator with God; you allow Spirit to direct all things. To fully live for your Higher Self means always holding on to Unconditional Love, while releasing all outcomes based on Judgment.

Very few individuals obtain this state on this earth. Many people find some blend between Ego and Higher Self, and feel that they are living for God. While it is true that every Soul is existing for God in every minute, if you cannot surrender 100 % of your Ego, you are still empowering it. Ego is so proficient at its job that it will lead you to incorrectly believe that everything is perfect, and that there is no need to do anything more than what you are presently doing. It has been said that the greatest trick the Devil ever played was to convince Man that he does not exist. Just substitute the word

"Ego" for "Devil" and you will begin to understand why it is so hard to recognize Real Truth.

To understand Real or Ultimate Truth, you must always remember that it is up to you to open to something greater than the Ego Self. The alternative is to remain lost within the prison of your own mind. This is not the true purpose of your life here.

Again, the purpose of Soul is to create and develop its Awareness, and then to serve as a co-creator with God in order to expand Creation at every level. Every Soul is serving a purpose in every moment, regardless of its level of Awareness. The capacity to understand our creations is directly related to our level of Consciousness, as well as our willingness to move beyond creating for the Ego Self. Creation goes way beyond the physical worlds.

There are worlds upon worlds, and Dimensions within Dimensions. God made Creation to be eternal and ever expanding. Since Creation is built from Consciousness, it will expand only when Souls expand it. When a Soul accepts a higher level of understanding as a Reality of experience, it will actually have that experience. The experience will become Real. You are, in this moment, no less than that which you can become. It is your belief that you are "only human" that holds you back.

The experiences that you are creating, or have been creating for lifetimes, serve as opportunities for you to expand your Consciousness. At any given time, you are the summation of all your prior experiences from the time of the birth of your Soul (i.e., the beginning of Creation). Please remember that the physical worlds are a training ground for Soul, and that most Souls that are here have had the experiences necessary to elevate themselves beyond this world. There are also Souls here, in this physical world, that are from the Higher Worlds. These Souls are here to help the less-evolved Souls find their way. This help or cooperation between worlds (Dimensions) holds true in every level of God's Creation. As noted previously, all of Creation is connected and interconnected through an infinite Matrix.

There are some Souls that find the physical worlds fulfilling; they will stay in them for thousands and thousands of years. It is up to each Soul to decide where it wishes to be within Creation. As you surrender to your Higher Self, you will have a greater understanding of the I Am and will be afforded greater opportunities to serve. I hope these Truths will become ever clearer to you, and that you will allow yourself the experience of living in Unconditional Love. Until then, however, you will remain somewhat blinded to True Reality, and will be seeing things through the filter of human sight.

The Human Experience: An Overview

A time to love, and a time to hate; a time for war, and a time for peace. What gain has the worker from his toil? I have seen the business that God has given to the sons of men to be busy with.

Eccles 3:8-10

Here, Ecclesiastes is describing the journey of Soul.

Your experience here on this earth for the most part is created within your own mind, but that is not where it ends. Beyond this physical world, you exist as Consciousness. In terms of True Reality, you are multidimensional.

Earlier you read that God is Spirit, and that those who worship him must worship him in Spirit and in Truth. Here, Spirit refers to the Consciousness that goes beyond Form. God is that which is formless. You, and everything else that exists, is part of the formless energy known as Consciousness. (Note that the term "consciousness" has a different meaning in common use. Usually, it denotes having full use of one's physical senses and does not apply to true spiritual awareness. Here, however, it refers to that which is infinitely Aware.)

God alone exists. From a Trinitarian viewpoint, we might say that the Father created Creation in three parts, the Father, the Son, and the Holy Spirit. In an individual sense, then, you are a Consciousness, within a Consciousness, existing within yet another Consciousness. This is a simple explanation of a very complex system. The most important point in understanding the concept of the Trinity is that there is a division of an indivisible Consciousness. This paradox will always remain a mystery to the mind of Man.

> *"Each Soul is on a unique journey, experienced at various levels of Consciousness ."*

Creation is where you can experience that which will lead you back to full Awareness. It is based on Consciousness. Each Soul is on a unique journey, experienced at various levels of Consciousness. Before you can move past the physical worlds, you must evolve to a level of Consciousness that can see past them. What you have experienced, in this life and all others, makes up your Consciousness. Your experiences are preparing you to elevate your Consciousness beyond this world.

Each Soul is able to reach the level that it has allowed itself to evolve to. The physical worlds provide many of the tools necessary for the individual Soul's evolution. They were created for Soul to experience in order to become more familiar with God. Getting to know the God-Self (the Higher Self) is essential to your evolution.

The evolution of Soul is something that happens out of choice; the greater your understanding, the greater your opportunity to consciously choose. Your rate of speed in developing Consciousness is directly related to the choices that you make. Whether you are looking at the Collective or the individual Consciousness, it is *Soul* that moves Creation.

Within the (core) Consciousness of each Soul is the desire to return home. Along with this desire, each Soul contains an Ego that is working to create a permanent home here in this world. This world was made for Ego, and Ego is a master at using itself to manipulate you and keep you living in illusion. Ego is so prevalent in this world that most Souls have trouble remembering that this is only a temporary experience. You have a much higher purpose for being here!

Remember, Ego will use your mind to convince you that what you are creating is Real. Indeed, everything that you experience is real to you until you change your perception of it. For example, look at the pain you feel over guilt. How long does it last? There is no set time. It will last as long as you cause it to last. You hold the responsibility for your every thought. You are the creator of your experiences!

You must become vigilant with your choices by becoming a Conscious creator. You read above that your Consciousness is divided into three parts, and that all parts make up the whole. Ego is powerful, but it cannot overcome the I Am—if the I Am exercises its authority by choosing to create from the Higher Self. There is always choice.

For the most part, your creations are part Ego and part Higher Self. There are, however, other factors, such as Karma, the Collective Consciousness, and the whole of Creation, that can influence and interconnect with your experiences. Creation is constantly shifting and adjusting to the changes in vibration.

The circumstances of your life were not brought about by accident. Before you were born, you decided what kind of life you would live. You chose the circumstances—things like your sex, your family, etc.—according to spiritual laws. This entire life experience is really nothing new to you. You have gone through it many times before, and you will continue to go through it until you reach Atonement Consciousness.

The Journey of Soul

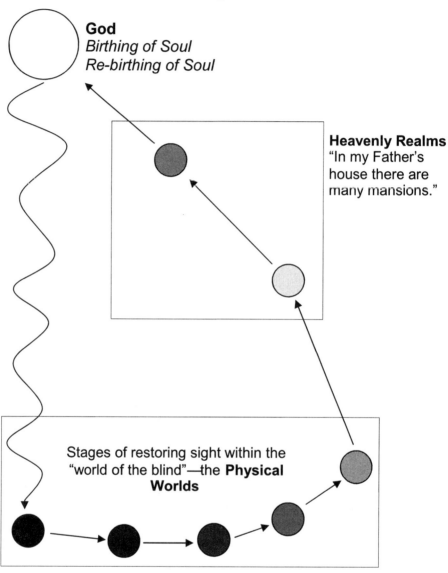

God
Birthing of Soul
Re-birthing of Soul

Heavenly Realms
"In my Father's house there are many mansions."

The Fall from Grace—the Soul is Spiritually Blinded

Stages of restoring sight within the "world of the blind"—the **Physical Worlds**

<u>Key</u>

- Ego; the Human Mind
- Blended states of Consciousness
- Spiritually Awakened

Reality comprises infinite realities of experience. At any given moment, there exist infinite potential experiences available to be experienced. All potential exists within Creation. Which experience is more real than any other?

From personal observation, we know that right now someone is dying, someone is being born, someone is getting married, someone is getting divorced, someone is buying a new car, someone is coming into God Consciousness, someone is committing murder, etc. I think that you would agree that the possibilities are endless. So, where do these realities come from? Is God setting up all these circumstances in our lives?

In spite of what you may have been taught, God the Father does not cause anything to happen in your life which is outside of Perfect Love. Individually and collectively, you cause everything else. This is why Reality is, in fact, realities—because each Soul is living its own version of Reality.

It is An Individual Journey

If there is only one Truth, why aren't the rules the same for everyone? The rules are not different for different individuals, but everything is relative to one's level of Awareness. What one person might accept as a positive experience, another might find negative. This is because everyone is viewing things based on his own idea of what this life means at any given moment.

Everyone's take on reality is unique. It exists within the individual's Consciousness. The only way your perception of anything can change is when *you* change it. To change your perception means you must consciously move outside of that which you are experiencing. You must view it as an observer. You must recognize that *you exist as different states of Consciousness simultaneously*. As long as you limit yourself to your Ego mind by believing that you are only Human, you will feel that you are at the mercy of forces outside of yourself. From that level of belief, it would be impossible for you to ever awaken from the dream that you have accepted as Real.

Fortunately, though, the Father saw this possibility and created a way out. The Holy Spirit can lead us out of the Darkness and back to the Light. New Agers call this Consciousness, begotten of God, the Universe itself. Whatever you may call it, you must look beyond your own Ego mind to find Truth.

Ultimately, the Truth that sets a Soul free from its self-created illusions must come from within, by means of a re-connecting to a more expansive Consciousness. No one can make your choice for you. Do not allow someone else's beliefs to prevent you from seeking your own connection. I cannot stress this strongly enough; it is one of the central ideas that God has instructed me to convey to you.

If you allow yourself to be limited by others' opinions, you are imposing their limitations on your spiritual growth. There is no one teaching, and no one person, that can magically transform you. You must bring yourself to your own awakening. You begin by becoming willing to accept a change in how you view things. Once begun, everything begins to change form. Much like the transformation of a caterpillar into a moth, the transformation from Ego based experiences to Spiritual ones happens over time.

While it is true that certain feelings and emotions can be shared, each Soul's journey is unique. Just as no two fingerprints are alike, no two journeys are the same. Through the various choices made, each Soul creates its own experiences, and they can only be fully shared with God the Father.

Just as there are exceptions to almost every rule, there is an exception to what can be shared with another. That exception is Love. Unconditional Love is the only True Reality that exits. Whenever you are sharing Unconditional Love you are eliminating the walls of separation and fully connecting to another.

6. Love: The Ultimate Treasure

What is so precious and valuable that some have abandoned all else to acquire it, while others have gone so far as to give up fortunes, or have even killed for it? What could be worth so much that people have been willing to sacrifice their lives for it? The answer is *Love*, that intangible, elusive, indefinable something we all strive for.

Throughout history, Love has been a driving force influencing the unfolding of events. However, in spite of the fact that Love is so important and so powerful, most of us have missed its real meaning.

Jesus said:

Love your enemies and pray for those who persecute you...

Mt 5:44

In a world of chaos, is such advice possible? Can we simple turn the other cheek and not seek revenge when we are unjustly attacked? To many, this sounds ludicrous, and outright stupid. They believe, instead of turning the other cheek, the correct or proper response to an attack is another blow. Enough force might deter further assaults from the enemy.

Obviously, there are distinct differences between these two approaches. Why would Jesus have made such a statement? Was he crazy, or did he know something that we are not aware of?

When Christ spoke of Love, do you suppose he was speaking of it as Man sees or defines it? You will find an answer to that question in the Bible. The Bible states that God is Love. Could that be true? Could that be the real meaning of Love? And if God is Love…what happened to this world?

Love is the Universal Truth

The Center of All Things

Although Love is at the core or center of all things, very few have even attempted to examine the meaning of this word. In fact, the understanding of most people is so limited and distorted that they can only see things directly related to their personal lives. By holding on to such distorted views, we make it impossible to see anything else. To see the real meaning of Love, we must open ourselves to something greater than our human minds, which are centered on the personal meaning of things.

The concept of the personal has also led to many incorrect beliefs; these beliefs became the dogmas/guidelines of some religions. Once the personal is accepted over the principle of God, all understanding of Truth in Love disappears or becomes distorted.

Ask a thousand people to give you their definition of Love, and you may get a thousand different answers. This is because they are responding from the human condition, which sees things in a distorted way.

The Bible says that God is Love; it also says that God is that which never changes. If both of these statements are true, how is it that Man's idea of Love/God is so different for everyone? Very few in this world truly recognize that, regardless of race, color, or creed, everyone comes from and is in fact part of the same Oneness. This Truth has been buried by personal desire. Love has escaped us, remaining behind a man-made veil of perception and supposition.

Hidden within all religions there is a universal Truth, a Truth so vast that it answers questions pertaining, not only to life as you perceive it, but also to Life as it actually is...a Truth that sets forth the difference between death as you perceive it and Death as it actually is. In this world, there exists such an intertwining of the perceived and the actual that there are times when the same definition has been used to describe both states.

While searching for Truth, the Seeker has often been left with the daunting task of defining the indefinable. This is the reason I wrote this book, and is the primary reason I am in this world.

Things are Not Always As They Seem

How many times have you experienced something, only to find out later that what you thought was true was actually erroneous? Have you ever experienced the feeling that you understood something—and yet still felt there was something missing? I have been there, and I know that you have been or will be there, too.

Opening yourself to understanding God and God's Creation beyond this physical world can be a Reality for you. To do otherwise is to miss out on Life. Those who opt to remain blind to the real meaning of Love will always find the world a mystery. They will continue to fumble in the dark.

Christ's message of Love fell mostly on deaf ears, but not because of the message's meaning. When Jesus spoke of loving your neighbor as yourself, he was attempting to teach that all people come from the same source, and are in fact part of the one Living God. God exists and experiences itself through being connected and interconnected to the whole of Creation. God is a single unified Consciousness, expressing itself in an infinite array of levels of Awareness. Creation is God, and God is Creation. To understand this better, remember that God is Love.

Love is the common thread that weaves through the tapestry of Creation. When you fully understand Love, you will know God. You cannot know one without knowing the other. They are One. Everything that happens within Creation is directly related to Love. Every emotion that exists is an aspect of it; in essence, Fear is simply a cry for Love. There is a fine line between Love and Fear. This is why the love we have for the most significant people in our lives can vacillate so greatly.

Real Love Never Changes

Have you ever heard someone say, "I used to love this or that person, but I no longer do so"? Such a statement comes from Judgment, and is not real Love. The emotion that Ego calls "love" is no more than a response based upon learning, observation, and conditioning. Shakespeare says, "All the world's a stage, and all the men and women merely players." For those living in Ego, this is a true statement. They are playing a role and living according to how they think they should live, instead of dropping all Judgment and living fully present in their hearts.

The Love to which Christ called us is not something that is easily learned or taught; to understand it fully it must be experienced within, by releasing the Judgment of all things in this world.

In this Ego-based world, everything that is viewed with the mind will be limited. Emotions such as fear, anger, jealousy, envy, hatred, depression, etc. are all viewed by the mind, and stand as obstacles to be overcome. All of these

"The Love to which Christ called us is not something that is easily learned or taught."

emotions are aspects of Love. While it is true that at times they can provide opportunities for greater understanding, no piece can take the place of the whole.

God is the Totality of the Whole, and yet all the parts have a place within that whole. How would you know what Unconditional Love is, without experiencing all the emotions that place conditions on Love?

So how do you understand Love? You begin by first understanding the system of Creation as God created it. Once this is understood, you must take the personal responsibility for your own unfolding or progression. If you allow limited thought to stand in your way, you cannot move beyond the barrier you have erected.

The self-imposed limitation is the only thing that can create the experience of Separation from God's Love. You are only capable of experiencing that which you allow yourself to experience. God's Love is Unconditional and ever-present. You grow in Consciousness through the experiences that you create. As you grow toward Atonement Consciousness, you will come to know what it means to Love without conditions.

Unconditional Love must be experienced before it can be given to others. It is only possible when you are living fully present in the moment, without any Judgment from your mind. The second that you move into your mind, you will be limiting yourself to an aspect of love based on human emotion, and you will lose sight of the whole. The human mind is limited by what you have experienced in this lifetime; therefore, if you have not experienced Unconditional Love in this lifetime, your human mind will not recognize it.

The heart is your core Consciousness. It is unlimited. It is the I Am of your Soul. Without the illusions of the Ego, the essence of the I Am is pure Unconditional Love, i.e., pure Consciousness (Atonement).

To better understand the process that occurs each time you embrace one emotion over another, look at the spectrum of colors. Each color exists as electromagnetic energy and operates at its own frequency. When you equally combine all the primary colors, you get the color white. White represents pure Consciousness. So it is with Love. When you can experience all emotion equally without a judgment, you are in the vibration of Love. Conversely, when one color or one emotion is more prevalent than the others, you will not have the purity of the whole.

Unconditional Love (God) is not the absence of emotions; it is the combination of all emotions in perfect harmony. Perfect harmony is that which is beyond Judgment. When Jesus spoke of peace, it was this state of connectedness that he was referring to.

If you want true lasting peace, not as the world might see it but a True Infinite Peace, then Unconditional Love is the treasure you have been seeking.

> *Peace I leave with you; my peace I give to you; not as the world gives do I give to you. Let not your hearts be troubled, neither let them be afraid.*
> Jn 14:27

There is a way to overcome all Fear. That way has been and will always be the same (see 1 Jn 4:18). Perfect Love (God) is the most powerful force, and it is above everything else.

7. Judgment and Karma

What is Judgment, and how does it apply to you? Let us return to the New Testament for some guidance.

> *Jesus said, "For judgment I came into this world, that those who do not see may see, and that those who see may become blind."*
>
> Jn 9:39

This means that he was here to present an understanding of things as they really are, and not as Man thinks they are. Remember that God created out of Love, there is no judgment in Love, and Love is still at the center of all things. God is not judgmental; Jesus clearly stated that the Father would not judge anyone.

> *The Father judges no one, but has given all judgment to the Son...*
>
> Jn 5:22

Many have misinterpreted this to mean that they will stand before Jesus and that he will judge them, assessing whether they did what they were called to do. Jesus specifically addressed this point when he declared he would judge no man:

> *I have come as light into the world, that whoever believes in me may not remain in darkness. If any one hears my sayings and does not keep them, I do not judge him; for I did not come to judge the world but to save the world. He who rejects me and does not receive my sayings has a judge; the word that I have spoken will be his judge on the last day.*
>
> Jn 12:46-48

How does this affect our lives and our destiny? Are you going to experience Heaven or Hell? Have you truly been saved? Is it enough to simply believe in Jesus to assure your salvation? All of these questions are answered when you fully understand Jesus' message, the *Word*. This is indeed essential to your salvation.

> *Jesus said to him, "I am the way, and the truth, and the life; no one comes to the Father, but by me."*

Jn 14:6

For those who do not do the will of the Father, there is no salvation. Within a perfect system that needs no judge or jury, it is your heart, not your mind, which sets the stage for your next experience. Many will be greatly disappointed to find that they have missed the chance to free themselves. Jesus never promised to do your work; he made it perfectly clear that each person is responsible for his or her own salvation.

Judgment is something that most people hold within themselves. They use it to evaluate everything and everyone in their lives. This standard determines what will come next. In every moment, we are either experiencing Love or we are learning lessons that can lead us there. Each moment can be experienced as Heaven or Hell, and this always relates to, and stems from, your attachment to your personal Judgment.

Why Would You Create Struggle?

As I have already mentioned, this life provides the opportunity for you to awaken yourself to God, by means of creating and then experiencing your creations. The circumstances in your life were not brought about by accident, but rather orchestrated through the rest of Creation via the Holy Spirit.

Before you were born, you were given a choice to decide what kind of life you would live. You made decisions concerning your physical makeup, your abilities, your country; you even decided the family you would be born into. All of these decisions were yours to make—and you made them, knowing full well that you were moving into an experience that would develop your Soul. Moreover, this experience of living is nothing new to you; you have gone through it many times, and you will continue to go through it until you reach Atonement Consciousness.

Each Soul has created the life it is living through the choices it has already made. So why would anyone create a life of poverty and struggle while another creates a life of luxury, and yet another creates a life that ends in a few months? These questions can only be answered when you view them through your (Soul) Consciousness, not through your human mind.

The Cycle of Karma

The life you are living is connected to the past lives that you have had. Just as in this moment you are a summation of all you have experienced in this life, you are also a summation of all your past lives. The I Am of your Soul stores and carries the memory of every experience you have ever had. Your past experiences will always play a role in your creations in terms of available energy. The energy available is proportionate to your level of Awareness. In this world, most people are limited to balancing the energies that they have embraced through wrong choices. While living with a judgmental mind, no one can escape the consequences of his thoughts.

Surely, you have heard the saying, "What you sow you shall reap." The Law of Cause and Effect states that for every action there is a reaction. Simply put, this is Karma.

You begin a cycle of Karma every time you act upon a human emotion. When you choose to create from Ego, you set energies in motion that bring about experiences. The experience resulting from your original thought presents yet another choice: to react from the level of Fear, or to interact from the Awareness of Love (God). If you react from Fear (that which comes from human emotion), you cause yet another imbalance within a harmonic system that must be rectified; the cycle continues. This cycle will continue indefinitely until you withdraw yourself from it, by foregoing the will of your Ego and choosing to serve God instead.

Once something is created via thought, it requires energy to fuel its development. When you, someone, or a group stops fueling a creation, the energies will start to diminish and your creation will change form. A good analogy is the building of a home. You must put a lot of attention and energy into the construction of your home, starting with the clearing of a space. Next, you work on setting a good foundation, followed by the framing of the sides; then you must work on the roof, in order to prevent the rains from coming in and destroying everything. What do you suppose would happen if you abandoned the construction of your home before it was complete? If you were to do that, all the effort you put into it would go to waste. The structure would deteriorate. The elements would start to wear away the building; eventually the walls would fall and the foundation would crack.

The point here is that what you put into your mind is what you will experience. You always have choice to create whatever you want, and the more focused attention you give to something, the stronger it becomes. You control what you will bring to yourself. No one can force you to do anything. *You are free.* Free to choose to live for this world, or free to elevate your Consciousness beyond this world.

If you choose to elevate to the point of realizing God, you must learn to love with divine Unconditional Love. You must have the willingness to see everyone and everything as God. You must develop control over the lower emotions such as greed, envy, lust, anger, etc. The more you allow Ego to rule your thoughts, the deeper you will bury your Awareness in darkness; you will stop its development or, in some cases, reverse the growth you have achieved.

Through the choices you make, you are setting the stage for your next life. This cycle will go on and on until you break it. The only way to break it is to choose Perfect Love and create from your Higher Self. Once you have surrendered your life (the Ego's will) to God, you become a co-creator. During these times of co-creation, you no longer accumulate any new Karma to deal with. Conversely, when you live for Ego you create Karma.

"Through the choices you make, you are setting the stage for your next life."

You carry with you any and all Karma that you have accumulated in prior lifetimes. Before moving on to higher worlds, you must deal with all of your Karma. It is up to each Soul to decide when (but not how) it will deal with its Karma. While the precise details are not given to you to work out, you *are* given great latitude over some of the circumstances or opportunities that will be available to you.

Many times a Soul will choose to be born into a particular family in order to work off some of the negative Karma that it has created with one or more family members in a previous lifetime. It is not uncommon for Souls to continue to form relationships with people they had been previously related to. With this understanding, we see that what we might perceive as struggle in our minds is, in fact, just part of a process of evolution.

The Balance of Energy & Polarity

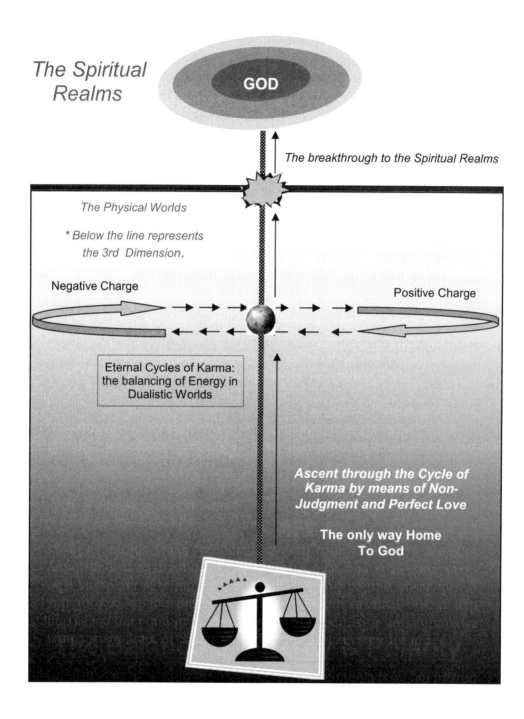

The Spiritual Realms

GOD

The breakthrough to the Spiritual Realms

The Physical Worlds

* Below the line represents the 3rd Dimension.

Negative Charge

Positive Charge

Eternal Cycles of Karma: the balancing of Energy in Dualistic Worlds

Ascent through the Cycle of Karma by means of Non-Judgment and Perfect Love

The only way Home To God

Man has been taught and conditioned to believe that he is separate from God. This idea of Separation leads to living a life of Fear. How much time do you spend feeling as though you are being tested to see if you measure up? God is not testing you. In fact, it is the thought that you are being tested that will create a test. As you elevate your Consciousness, you will see that what you once took to be negative may now be positive. Did the rules change—or your perceptions?

While on the subject of perception, this may be good time to talk a little about the reality and the myths of reincarnation.

Reincarnation

To properly understand reincarnation, you must first understand what life is. Life is God in expression. Because God is infinite, having no beginning and no end, life itself has no beginning and no end. With this in mind, you can begin to understand that *death cannot exist* in terms of True or Ultimate Reality.

What is death, then, if not Real? Death is a temporary experience that has no particular duration. It can be experienced for as briefly (or as long) as one holds on to the belief that it is Real. Earlier, you read that Death did not originate with God, but rather with Man. The Bible states that by "a man came death, therefore by a man also came the resurrection from death" (1 Cor 15:21). Man could not restore something permanent, such as a Real Death. This resurrection was really a restoring of understanding in Life (God).

Each Soul must go through its own unique journey—this is the basis of reincarnation. Within the system of Creation, there are many Dimensions to be explored. In this realm, you are given different opportunities to develop your Awareness of God. Until you reach the necessary level of understanding, you will continue to experience different incarnations in this world, not as a new life with a new beginning, but rather as a continuation of your one Life.

In terms of this world, you are always subject to (and tied to) any energy you have touched. Karma is the way in which the system of Creation restores this energy to a perfect state of balance. Hinduism and Buddhism refer to the cycle of birth and death as a wheel. The only way to stop the wheel is to choose Perfect Love.

What is Sin?

Simply put, Sin is anything that causes you to feel separate from God. I was raised as a Christian, and taught to believe that we were all created in Sin. I was also taught that, unless I accepted Jesus Christ as my Savior, I was destined to go to Hell and burn for all of eternity. I, like many others, have found it hard to believe that God would create Souls only to condemn them to eternal damnation. This teaching never made sense to me. If you are saved or reborn merely by accepting Jesus Christ as your Savior, where does responsibility fit in?

God created Souls with Free Will. This means you are free to *be*. Free to choose. Do you really think that Buddha, Muhammad and Confucius are burning in Hell for eternity, simply because they did not outwardly proclaim Jesus Christ as their Savior? Of course not.

In fact, all these Masters had the same message. Each was teaching Love as he understood it. Each spoke of detachment from Ego-related thoughts and beliefs. They may have expressed themselves differently or used different words, but the message (vibration) was essentially the same. Every Master walks with a Consciousness that is beyond this world. It is difficult for those who choose to limit their Awareness to the things of this world to fully understand their message, but their Truth has endured for thousands of years.

Your level of understanding of Sin is directly related to how much Ego-based Consciousness you have. If you sit quietly and are honest with yourself, you will feel in your heart where you are in

Consciousness. Do you see things through the eyes of Perfect Love, or are some things still viewed from a fearful mind?

Whenever you are faced with a choice, your decision will be based on the summation of all that you are, or have been, up to that moment. Let's say you are walking down the road and find a wallet with a thousand dollars in it. I think that you already have a good idea of what you would do with that wallet right now, before you even stop to think about it. Why is that? Because, if you are truthful, you will correctly identify yourself within your own mind. You know that you will do one of two things. Either you will serve your Lower Self and think of what you can do with that money, or you will serve your Higher Self and try to give it back to the person who lost it.

Keep in mind that what you are in this moment is not necessarily what you will be tomorrow. It is possible for you to see yourself as one thing now and something very different later. This is one of the greatest messages that the Masters taught. You must free yourself of this world in order to see beyond its limits and attain True Awareness.

If you continue to evolve your Awareness, you will come to know that Sin is nothing more than a perception based on Judgment, a perception that causes you to experience Separation from God.

Guidelines for Living

In this world, Soul is at many different levels of Awareness. It needs some form of guidance. You have already seen that there has been an evolution of Consciousness, and along that path there have been rules applying to, and appropriate for, certain times. At one time, the highest Truth that Man's Consciousness could accept was a simple one stating, "An eye for an eye." As the level of the Collective Consciousness evolved, the Truth became more elevated.

Everyone on this planet holds his own set of values. These values come from the memories of every experience, from this life and previous ones. What you might find offensive, someone else might accept as perfectly fine. This is because you judge things based on your own *unique* experiences. In each society, there are behavioral guidelines. They have been with us for thousands of years; they serve to maintain order.

Moses received the Ten Commandments. The Buddha taught the Four Noble Truths and the Eightfold Path. Common to most religions and philosophies is some form of the Golden Rule:

- Buddhism: *"Do not hurt others in ways that you yourself would find hurtful."*

- Christianity: *"Whatever you wish that men would do to you, do so to them."*

- Judaism: *"That which is hateful to you, do not to your fellow man."*

- Hinduism: *"This is the sum of duty: Do nothing to others which would cause pain if done to you."*

- Islam: *"Not one of you is a believer until he desires for his brother that which he desires for himself."*

- Taoism: *"Regard your neighbor's gain as your own gain, and your neighbor's loss as your loss."*

- Zoroastrianism: *"That nature alone is good which keeps from doing unto another whatever is not good for itself."*

When you remember that you are an individualized aspect of pure Consciousness, a Son begotten of the living Father, and that the universe gives you exactly what you are asking for without Judgment, you will understand that *whatever you do for another you are really doing for yourself.*

As you continue to choose to develop your Awareness, this Truth will become crystal clear. Eventually, you will be moved to live with no other desire but to serve God's will. It is God's will that you remember and teach others that you are, in fact, the same Unconditional Love that you came from and always have been.

Until Unconditional Love becomes your Reality, you will still be creating from Ego-based thought. You will then need some sort of guideline for living. When you have the eyes to see and the ears to hear, it will be time for you to elevate beyond this world and move past the limitations imposed on you by such guidelines.

To go home to God—to move past the levels of Creation that exist in this world of Illusion—you must be pure of heart. There cannot be the slightest bit of Judgment left in your Consciousness. While you are living in your Ego, there is Judgment and a need for Judgment. Until such time that you become so pure that there is no form of Judgment within you, you will be dealing with your Ego. And when you are in your Ego, there is no one to judge you except yourself.

"You Shall Have No Gods Before Me"

This commandment speaks for itself. If there is anything in your life that you place before God—including yourself—you have broken the First Commandment.

For all those who were taught, as I was, to view Jesus Christ as your Savior, it is time to reevaluate your thinking. I am not saying that if you were to emulate Jesus you would not be free of this world. Jesus wanted Souls to emulate him, but it is not Jesus who saves you—it is you who saves you! You must take responsibility for your salvation. Since time immemorial, every spiritual Master has taught this. *It is All One Truth.*

Atonement Consciousness

To atone means to make amends or reparation for wrongdoing, or to bring into agreement. This definition is appropriate for two levels of Awareness. Making amends could represent forgiveness, both in yourself and in others. The second part of the definition moves beyond the need for forgiveness.

The higher meaning of Atonement is the state where all things come together as One within your Consciousness. It is the point where there is no longer any need to see things as good or bad, black or white, positive or negative. All forms of Judgment disappear. Atonement is also where the I Am of your Soul embraces both the Ego and the Higher Self, and recognizes them as part of the whole. All ideas of Separation of self disappear.

This is, of course, an attainable Consciousness for each one of us. It is the Truth of who we are.

It must, however, be your choice to see that Truth. Choosing to see a Higher Truth means viewing your experiences with the eyes of Soul rather than with the eyes of Man; it means making that Higher Truth your Reality. This can be accomplished only by surrendering the will of your Ego to your Higher Self.

The Soul's purpose is much higher than living for this world. Once you reach Atonement Consciousness (the mind of Christ), you will understand what it means to be not of this world. Everything will take on a new meaning. You will only be concerned with your relationship to God. The greater the surrender, the greater the development, and the greater the role that Soul will play within the system. As mentioned previously, no Soul has been created differently then any other; it is only through surrender of Ego self that they can reach this goal.

Of all the false beliefs that you may hold, the most devastating is the belief that the Creator is a God of Judgment who is waiting to punish you for your wrongful acts. As a child, I often had images or ideas of how things should be. When the moment flowed in a different direction, I would ask God what I did wrong—as though I were being punished for something I did or said.

Like many children in this country, I was taught that God was judgmental, and that we lived in a world of reward and punishment. I subscribed to the false belief that God was watching and weighing every action we performed, and constantly keeping records to see if we measured up. While there is truth in the fact that we are responsible for our every thought, and there is indeed a consequence for every action, it is not true that God is there to judge us.

"It is not true that God is there to judge us."

There is never a time when our Father is anything but Unconditionally Loving. Anyone who understands the concept of Unconditional Love knows that it is impossible for God to be judgmental.

8. Detachment

Going Beyond the Limits

For those who would wish to expand their vision, willingness to release all thoughts of limitation is a prerequisite! Any thought that pertains to the world of Form puts a restriction on what you can experience.

The Bible, like many other holy scriptures, contains Truth. However, once the Ego gets involved, Truth is pushed aside to make room for personal agendas. This is why I would advise everyone never to settle for someone else's interpretation of Truth. Each Soul must find its own Truth. The Buddha (the Enlightened One) knew this. He said:

Do not believe everything that you have been told, just because your parents believed it before you and their parents before them. Look within, and if you find that it is True there, then for you it is True.

The Sufi Master Rumi agreed:

No man can lend his vision to another.

Each of us is going to experience only what we *allow* ourselves to experience, and for most of us, what is experienced is not Reality but a self-made distortion. Hard as this may be to accept, it happens to be the case. We are all in charge of how much or how little we can experience, based on the amount of Light/ Love we embrace. Yes, this is a world of darkness, but there is always an infinite amount of Light available; this Light is not obvious to the average person, due to his preoccupation with perceived reality.

If you do not fast to the world, you will not find the kingdom; if you do not keep the Sabbath as Sabbath, you will not see the Father.

Thom 27

Fasting from the world is not an easy thing. You will be tempted repeatedly to use your intellect to make sense of what is in front of you. When this happens, remind yourself that the eyes of Man are the eyes of Fear (Separation), and the eyes of Spirit (God) are the eyes of Love (Oneness). Fear is the predominant force in this world; almost every thought and belief here has its roots in Fear, including our common idea of love. The human mind cannot accept anything that it cannot relate to from past experience.

> *When you see your likeness, you rejoice. But when you see your images which came into existence before you, which neither die nor are made manifest, how much will you bear?*

Thom 84

Here Jesus is saying that Egos (personalities) are happy to see each other, but when they meet a Spiritual presence they cannot cope. Based on my personal experience, most people will want to run away from you as soon as you begin moving into Higher Truth. This is the natural reaction when a bright Light is cast upon a dark heart that lives in Fear. Sadly, unless your friends and relatives have moved beyond their Egos, they will most likely not be able to understand what you are experiencing. To most people, you are crazy to give up the things of this world and their temporary sense of security.

Nevertheless, you must look only to God for your Truth. If you cannot let go of your limited perceptions, then you are limiting yourself to the world of Ego. The Reality is that your Consciousness is not limited to this world. It is only your *perception* of limitation that creates the obstacle. It is a self-imposed obstruction. In Reality, there are no limits imposed on any Soul as to the degree of Awareness that can be attained.

The diagram on the following page illustrates some of the obstacles that can impede vision.

Boxes or Veils of Illusion

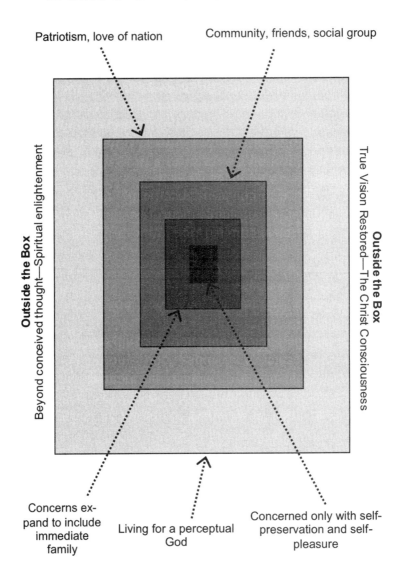

Patriotism, love of nation

Community, friends, social group

Outside the Box
Beyond conceived thought—Spiritual enlightenment

Outside the Box
True Vision Restored—The Christ Consciousness

Concerns ex-
pand to include
immediate
family

Living for a perceptual
God

Concerned only with self-
preservation and self-
pleasure

- *Development begins at the center of the diagram and moves up and out.*
- *Note that, at the center (the lowest point), the Light of Love (God awareness) does not penetrate the walls created in the mind of Man.*
- *True Vision is only experienced outside the boxes of Man's conceived beliefs.*

The Mechanics of Detachment

To truly understand detachment, you must agree that God is pure Consciousness (both within and beyond all Form), and that you are an extension of that Consciousness. With this in mind, you can see that detachment means letting go of all conditioned, limited, and preconceived ideas of this world. This involves establishing (or rather re-establishing) the connection to your Higher Mind, as opposed to your Ego mind.

This is an Ego-based world concerned with self-gratification. Self-gratification is sometimes a difficult thing to understand. There are times when you may think that you are living your life for God, while in fact you are still empowering your Ego. Everything in this world has the potential to keep you in the illusion of Separation. Your attachments are used by Ego to keep you in Fear, incapable of recognizing Love. Fear and Love operate at different vibrations; you cannot experience both at the same time.

Even though your Fears are an illusion, the pain that is created by them is a real experience to you. Your entire Ego life has revolved around satisfying perceived wants, desires, and the pleasures of your physical life. It doesn't matter what form your attachments take. An attachment to money is no different from an attachment to power or an attachment to a relationship. Attachment is attachment, and all attachment is Ego-based and limited.

All of the decisions you make for your human self are in some way self-serving. When your Ego asks God to create for you, it is always doing so based on what it believes to be true. This can create a great deal of pain, as the two states of Consciousness will clash directly.

Trying to understand what happens at that point with your mind is impossible. You will only find comfort and peace when you are expanded in Consciousness; for example, when you are meditating. The human mind is incapable of understanding that which it is unfamiliar with. The only time that you will truly know whether something is serving your Ego is when you *do not use your human mind*.

Each person deals with detachment according to the level of Awareness of his individual Soul. Some people unconsciously release their attachments and move beyond them quicker than others. Then there are those who have a desire to surrender to God, but find that their Egos will not let go. It will serve you well to remember that you are the only one determining what you will experience; all your experiences in this world follow your thoughts. Detachment can be as easy or difficult as you make it.

Many times, you will feel as though you are releasing the same thing repeatedly, until you finally realize that you still have an attachment to something that you thought had already been released. You have moved past something only when you are prepared to live without it. We must often lose that which we are attached to, *before* we see that we were indeed attached to it!

When you consciously choose God over self, you must be willing to surrender the will of your Ego to God's will. At that time, you will become awakened to the realization that you are One with God. You will leave behind the perceptions of your old life. You will experience a new beginning, a re-birthing from one level of Consciousness to another. This is what it truly means to be reborn.

What about attachments to things that cannot be seen or touched? Detachment from your false beliefs is hardest of all, but if it is your desire to move beyond this world, you must persevere. There is no easy way to Surrender. *Either you forsake all for God, or you remain in your Ego, blinded to True Reality*.

It is not an easy path. The Buddha put it this way:

Those that follow the Way might well follow the example of an ox that marches through the deep mire carrying a heavy load. He is tired, but his

> *steady, forward-looking gaze will not relax. O*
> *Monks, remember that passion and sin are more*
> *than the filthy mire, and you can escape misery*
> *only by earnestly and steadfastly preserving in the*
> *Way.*

And this is what Jesus said:

> *For the gate is narrow and the way is hard, that*
> *leads to life, and those who find it are few.*
> > Mt 7:14

If it is your desire to return home to God in Consciousness, you must be willing to make this commitment each day. No matter what comes up in your life, you must hold on to the vision, and stay on the straight and narrow path. Detachment is the key to your salvation; if you choose to move beyond this world, you must be prepared to give up the finite for the Infinite.

Living Fully Present in the Moment

The state of Pure Being is a level of Consciousness that is unfamiliar to most people. Pure Being means living in the vibration of Unconditional Love. It means going beyond all Ego thoughts. It cannot be experienced with your human judgmental mind.

Pure Being requires you to shift your Consciousness to a higher level. This level is that which transcends Time—it is the eternal moment of Now! If you stop to think about what you are experiencing, you will move back into your human mind and lose touch with the present moment.

Regarding the loss of True Vision which comes from Judgment, Rumi once said:

> *The eye goes blind when it only wants to see Why.*

To maintain this degree of detachment requires a great deal of practice. You will not achieve it without a great desire and willingness to achieve it. Most of us have been taught and conditioned to develop our minds, and our creations have reflected this conditioning. You must consciously choose to *elevate your Consciousness beyond the existing programs of your mind.*

It is helpful to remind yourself that other people are subject to the same conditioning you have received. They are usually not capable of understanding what it is to live in Pure Being. This does not mean that you cannot have relationships with them; but you cannot look to them for your Truth. You cannot live their version of Truth and think that you can maintain your own. Re-birthing of true Awareness is almost never an instantaneous thing that you can just jump into. You live in an Ego-based world. You must forego the Judgment of all people on this earth. You have to move past the desire to be accepted by others.

To live in the moment means to be not of this world in Consciousness. To maintain this expanded state of Awareness, you must continually see through the illusions of this world. The Spirit can continue to use the things of this world to achieve desired results, but it cannot be attached to anything or anyone. Any form of attachment will create some kind of Judgment, which will create limitations for you. You will not be able to experience pure, Unconditional Love in that moment.

The ecstasy of Pure Being is a natural state of your Soul's Consciousness. It is only your Ego that prevents you from experiencing it. It is okay to acknowledge your Ego as long as you know how to move beyond it. This is not easy, and it is not easy to recognize Truth if we believe that the illusions of our Ego are Real.

In Reality, God loves you Unconditionally. His Love is unalterable and is always available to you. God has never abandoned you; rather, you have closed yourself to God. Are you willing to say, "God, you have my full attention"?

You are Holy; yet, you are the one causing the experience of Separation from God. You alone can stake a claim to the divine, Pure Being already within you. This process is not moving you into a new state of Being. You are simply unveiling your original state. In it, you realize that to co-create with God is creating for the whole of Creation.

"God loves you Unconditionally; his Love is always available to you."

You and God are One. This same Truth has been available to Souls for thousands of years. Our beloved Brother Jesus came into this world to show us that it is possible to have an Ego and still be able to elevate our Consciousness. Jesus was the living example of one who loved God more than the Ego self.

9. Meditation

Be still, and know that I am God.

Ps 46:10

Meditation is the key to opening the door of Spirit. People give me strange looks when I tell them they can speak to God if they get their Ego out of the way. In order to break free of the control of Ego, you must be willing to break out of the limitations you have created in your mind. How are you going to do this? Meditation gets you beyond the human mind.

There has been a lot written about meditation. Many people feel that it is something to be feared. Meditation is not a "New Age" phenomenon; it has been around since the beginning of civilization. Have you ever had the experience of getting lost in thought, where time seemed to slip away? Have you ever had a daydream? These are examples of what meditation is all about. Meditation is moving beyond your Ego thoughts; in other words, it allows you to see without thinking.

Using Your Brain

But when you give alms, do not let your left hand know what your right hand is doing.

Mt 6:3

Here Jesus uses the hand to represent different states of Consciousness. It is interesting that he employs this metaphor, keeping in mind what we know now—namely, that the left side of the brain controls the right hand and the left hand is controlled by the right side of the brain. Yes, modern science has discovered that each side of the brain is in charge of a different state of Consciousness.

The left side of the brain is limited to logical linear functioning, and cannot deal with more than one thing or task at a time. It tends to forget a string of words or numbers rapidly. The right side of the brain has the overall view; it is capable of non-linear functioning. It can compare many things simultaneously, and its memory of pictures, feelings, and emotions is permanent.

Considering that the evolutionary development of Man was initially based on basic needs and survival, it is obvious that the left side of the brain had to be primary. It is not until one is free from the struggle of everyday life that the right side can be brought to the fore. Until that time, the right side is forced to remain in the background. Only during times of relaxed thought (such as meditation) can this shift take place.

I have had people tell me that the moment of awakening seems to be outside of their control, and is not a matter of choice. I can only say that, as seen from the perspective of the left side of the brain, they would be correct. Science has determined that the left side can only hold to the notion of the next sequential image. One would have to shift from the left side to the right side in order to transcend this limitation.

"Are you limited to and controlled by the brain, or are you using it?"

The essential question is: Are you limited to and controlled by the brain, or are you using it (as one might drive a car, for example)? The first premise would leave you powerless and without choice; the second would allow you to change your path, much like deciding to take an alternate route on a road trip.

Time for Some Exercise

Before moving on, try shifting from merely *seeing* words to *feeling* their vibration. By this, I mean using your imagination to create a picture beyond words. This perspective is necessary in order that you remain open, refusing to allow past judgments to govern or limit your experience.

It would be helpful if you could find a quiet place where you will not be disturbed for least five minutes. Now get as comfortable as you can. Shift your attention to your breathing. Take a deep breath; hold it as long as you can without feeling any discomfort. Now, gradually exhale through your mouth, while paying close attention to the different sensations you are feeling in the body. Repeat this process three more times. On the fourth inhalation, allow your sight to travel inward beyond the point of stopping at the lungs, remembering that, with each breath, you are bringing life-sustaining energy to feed every cell in that mechanism called your body.

If you practice this simple technique and allow your Consciousness to travel to every part of your body, you will not only be opening your inner eyes. You will be clearing away the blockages that cause most of the physical problems people experience in this world. This technique can be used to heal various problems and illnesses within the body; there are even documented cases where terminal illnesses have been overcome through such visualizations.

While the health benefits alone would warrant the time and effort you put into it, this simple exercise is designed to shift your sight from the limited outer world to the unlimited inner world. Its effectiveness will vary, depending on your desire and your ability to accept your inter-connection to All That Is (i.e., God). The more time you spend in this state, the greater your feelings of relaxation. If you allow it to happen, you will discover that there is another world that you have been too self-absorbed to see.

The Practice of Meditation

You are responsible for your own spiritual evolution. Wherever you have brought your Awareness to, here and now, is the level you start from when you leave this physical body. For those not yet familiar with their Higher Self or going beyond the mind, let us start with a simple meditation.

Clear your mind of preconceived images. Sit quietly. Try to release the distractions of everyday life. Now relax your body. This may be the first time that you have pulled your attention away from the outside world and have journeyed inward. Once in a relaxed state, you can try some simple exercises such as deep breathing, feeling your lungs expand and contract, or trying to feel your big toe. (You know that you can feel it if you try, because you could move it if you wanted to.)

For now, try to be aware of it without moving it. Don't be too concerned if the outside world diverts your attention. Actually, if the outside world does distract you, you will begin to understand why you have not allowed the development of your Higher Self. This world was intended either to be a place where the Soul can see God at every moment, or a place where you can live an illusion that will keep you in the dark forever.

There is a razor's edge between seeing through the eyes of Spirit and seeing through the eyes of Man. How else could Soul have the opportunity for growth? It was never meant to be easy or obvious for every Soul at every level of Awareness.

Back to your toe. Let's move up the body. Place your attention on your ankles. Can you feel them? Great! Continue this exercise until you can move your attention to wherever you want it to be. You can shift your focus to any point. The choice is yours!

Some yogis have developed control over their bodies to the point where they can stop their hearts. This is not that hard to understand when we see the body for what it is. Quite simply, the body is a machine that carries you around. You are Consciousness in a physical body. You can be aware or unaware that your Consciousness controls your body and its functions. What about when you are sleeping? Who is in control then?

You are so much more than the image that you have given yourselves or have allowed others to give you. Is an outside force controlling you, or are you in control? The truth is that you control *everything* in your life. Just as it takes your Consciousness to move your toe or your ankle, it takes your Consciousness to create the events or circumstances in your life. When Jesus said, "We were made in the image of God," he was right. God is the totality of all things, just as you are the total of the parts of your Consciousness.

This life is an opportunity for you to unfold your Awareness and move ahead on your journey home.

A short time before hearing the voice of God in the spring of 1996, someone told me that I should go back to meditation and prayer. Immediately I formed an image in my mind of what I believed this meant, and I stated that I had no time in my life for it.

I, like most men, was so busy playing the role of father, husband, and businessman, that I had no time for anything else— least of all meditation. Looking back on the moment, I now realize that I was confused over the exact meaning of meditation. Many people today are equally mystified. To them it is something that belongs to the New Age movement, and it has little or no appeal.

Speaking from my own experience, I can only tell you that it opened a whole new world. Today I recognize meditation as the key that unlocks the door to Higher Realms. Without that key, you will always maintain the same mind that has created and preserves erroneous beliefs, beliefs that veil True Reality.

Once understood, meditation is not something to be frightened of. It is rather something to be embraced and practiced. From the Bible, we know that meditation was not only practiced but recommended as something holy:

> *Blessed is the man who walks not in the counsel of the wicked, nor stands in the way of sinners, nor sits in the seat of scoffers; but his delight is in the law of the LORD, and on his law he meditates day and night.*
>
> Ps 1:1-2

Of all the things taught in all religions, there is nothing more important than meditation. In meditation, you go within for your connection to All That Is. To go within requires a willingness to lay aside, if only temporarily, all thoughts of this world, and a willingness to see for the first time with your inner eyes. Once activated, these inner eyes will open your vision to a whole new world.

In this world, it is sometimes difficult to discern Truth. If you wan to know Real Truth, God has pointed the way:

Be Still and Know That I am God!

10. Reality & The Common Thread

Beyond all Self-created perceptions, perceptions born and lived out within the human mind, resides Real or Absolute Truth. The only True Reality.

Many have claimed to discover this Truth. In most cases, what they have discovered is only an aspect of it. This has led to a great deal of confusion and conflict. Attachment to incomplete beliefs has often resulted in death, either by killing in the name of false religion or by sacrifice in its defense.

In a world dominated by false belief systems, one is confronted by two basic questions: What am I to believe? What is Real? You are going to need some guidance in sorting through these systems and assessing whether they represent Truth.

Here is my best advice. When considering conflicting religious truth claims, look first at how they describe the qualities of God. Do they limit that which has no limits? Let's refer back to the basic attributes of God:

1. *God is Omnipresent.*
    This means that God is present everywhere at all times, and is both seen and unseen, within and without. Did you ever consider that the water you drink or the air that you breathe falls into this category? God is in this world, and is in every other world, galaxy, universe, or Dimension.

2. *God is Omniscient.*
    God is all knowing and nothing can escape his awareness. Both in and beyond this world, God is aware of every detail, down to the position of every grain of sand in the desert.

3. *God is Omnipotent.*
    God is all-powerful and capable of changing anything or any circumstances within Creation.

Now while many say that they believe these qualities do indeed describe God, in their hearts they do not fully accept this. For instance, they will ask themselves, "If God is capable of changing everything, why does he allow so much injustice to exist in this world?"

According to the Bible, God is Unconditionally Loving. Given this, does it make sense that some people are born only to live a short life of misery and suffering, while others enjoy riches and privilege, gliding through a long, pleasure-filled existence? How can we believe in a God that can permit such cruelty and injustice? Is God truly cruel, vindictive, and unjust? The answer to these questions lies at the core of the major religions.

> *"There is a common thread that runs through all existence and interconnects all things."*

There is a common thread that runs through all existence and interconnects all things. It is the fabric of Creation. What is it? Love. The Love that *is* God.

This Love is not human. It is far greater. To understand it, you must go beyond mere physical experience, and discover a world that most of us miss entirely.

The Worlds Beyond

Remember when Jesus said that he was "in this world, but not of it"? If you look at the episode of the Transfiguration (Mt 17, Mk 9, Lk 9), you will see that Peter, James, and John witnessed a meeting between Jesus, Moses, and Elijah on a mountain. What made this meeting unusual was the fact that Moses had died some 1200-1500 years earlier, and Elijah some 900 years earlier. Clearly, this demonstrated that there is interaction between the various Dimensions within Creation. So there is more to this world than meets the eye!

All great religions teach that there is indeed more than we can physically see. They teach that our job here in this life is to develop ourselves, to become something more.

> *What is night for all beings is the time of awakening for the self-controlled; and the time of awakening for all beings is night for the introspective sage.*
>
> Purport: *There are two classes of intelligent men. The one is intelligent in material activities for sense gratification, and the other is introspective and awake to the cultivation of self-realization. Activities of the introspective sage, or thoughtful man, are night for persons materially absorbed. Materialistic persons remain asleep during such a night due to their ignorance of self-realization. The introspective sage, however, remains alert in that night of the materialistic men. Such sages feel transcendental pleasure in the gradual advancement of spiritual culture, whereas the man in materialistic activities, being asleep to self-realization, dreams of varieties of sense pleasure, feeling sometimes happy and sometimes distressed in his sleeping condition. The introspective man is always indifferent to materialistic happiness and distress. He goes on with his self-realization activities undisturbed by material reactions.*

Bhaktivedanta Swami, <u>Bhagavad-Gita As It Is</u>

Taoism teaches that all values and concepts are relative to the mind that entertains them. In order to experience True Reality, one is required to quiet the everyday thinking mind.

> *To the mind that is still, the whole universe surrenders.*
>
> <u>Tao te Ching</u>

At a time when there was dispute over which of the gods were to be worshipped in Arabia, Muhammad, the Prophet of Islam, declared *la illaha ill' Allah!*—there is no god but God! Where did this revelation come from? After many hours of meditation, Muhammad had a vision of the angel Gabriel, who assured him that he was a Messenger of God.

It would seem evident from these examples, drawn from varied religious traditions, that there are different levels of experience available. One level is human or physical; the other is Spiritual.

The Man Who Woke Up

The Buddha also realized that this world is asleep. A Hindu prince, he was born in 563 B.C. into a noble family in northern India. He was raised by an adoring father, who wanted to shield him from the sight and knowledge of anything unpleasant. He appeared to have everything anyone could want. He was a handsome man destined to inherit his father's throne. He married a princess and had a child. According to legend, one day he saw on the roadside a sick man, an aged man, and a corpse on a litter. Shocked by his first experience with the unfamiliar world, he lost all joy for living.

One night, while his family was sleeping, he set off for the forest. He renounced the world and all things to seek enlightenment. After years of meditation and inner searching, the Buddha discovered enlightenment.

Once people recognized that he had achieved inner peace, they asked him,

> *"What are you? Are you a God?"*
> *"No."*
> *"An angel?"*
> *"No."*
> *"A saint?"*
> *"No."*
> *"Then what* are *you?"*
> *He responded: "I am Awake."*

What all these teachers presented had its origin in another Dimension, a different version of the reality experienced here by almost all the human race.

The Course in Miracles

This book is a more recent communication from another realm. First, let me state that I am convinced that this book is a genuine and trustworthy revelation of Jesus Christ, as revealed through Professor Helen Schucman of Columbia University in the 1960s and 1970s. The *Course* underlines and expands upon almost all the ideas put forth in this book.

This being said, I would like to add something important: it is not easy to accept the precepts outlined in the *Course*. In fact, it is probably more difficult to understand the *Course* than it is to understand what you have read in this book, however difficult that may have been. In order to understand the *Course*, you are continually asked to interpret through the eyes of Spirit. In this world, few have developed these eyes sufficiently to comprehend the *Course.*

After being instructed by Spirit to write this book, I was invited to attend a study meeting on the *Course.* My first reaction was excitement. Wow! It seemed I was not alone; the words I heard resonated with the same Truth that I had been instructed to teach! I was also pleasantly shocked to find so many people with an interest in living for Spirit. I was told that there were groups that met in almost every city in the country.

Unfortunately, my exhilaration was brief. It did not take me long to realize that both teacher and students were not "awakened"; in fact, they were very confused. The questions that kept coming up clearly showed that no one present had a genuine understanding of True Reality. One time I asked a woman sitting next to me, "How long have you been attending these meetings?" Eight years, she said.

"Does one ever get this?"

I was dumbfounded. How is it possible to be confused about something after eight years of study? I found myself asking, Does one *ever* get this?

Seeking to answer that question, I continued to attend. Week after week after week, I heard the same Ego-based questions. Once in a while there appeared to be a breakthrough; it would seem that someone was on the verge of understanding! Then, inevitably, history would repeat itself. The person would return to the world of darkness once again, standing firm in representing Ego beliefs.

Dismayed by the continued stagnation of those around me, I tried several other groups. Sadly, it did not matter where I went: the same questions appeared time and time again. Where was the problem? Was it in the material? I read at random various parts of the book, looking for clues, yet I never found any contradiction that would lead to the widespread confusion I was witnessing.

I began attending three meetings a week at various locations. After several years of this, I realized that the problem was not in the *Course*, but rather in the unwillingness of its adherents to adopt its principles as Truth, to be lived and not just intellectualized. As with other forms of Truth presented in various religions, including Christianity, there were those who wished to interpret the *Course* to suit their own Ego's agenda, as opposed to taking it as it was given.

Christ instructed his disciples to be willing to forsake everything and everyone in this world. The *Course* is just as adamant on this point. Obviously, this is the opposite of the Ego's agenda. The Ego maintains that everything you believe about this world is valid, and as such, the world should be honored and preserved; modified, yes, but preserved. The Ego is quite proficient at the game, and will be happy to play along with your Spiritual search. Often the Ego will portray itself as the True Self. This leads people to believe that they are on the right path.

Years of observing those who purport to be Spiritual teachers has led me to this conclusion: They think they can have the best of both worlds. They have found a temporary solution to their troubles. By partially accepting Truth, they have adjusted their life views slightly. This in turn leads to a degree of solace. Moreover, many of the students seem to be satisfied to have a support group where they can share their pain.

In the long run, this kind of thinking will always get in the way of experiencing True Reality. The *Course* clearly teaches that enabling the Ego is not the answer; it will cost you True vision.

> *Either truth is apparent, or it is not. It cannot be partially recognized.*
>   A Course in Miracles (ACIM): Manual for
>   Teachers, 17 4:9-10

A gray area can exist only in a world founded in Judgment. In Reality, beyond the Dimensions of experience within Time,

Duality gives way to Perfect Love. The experience of Perfect Love, however, is not automatic.

According to the *Course*, one's sole responsibility is to recognize the illusion of the world of the Ego. God will honor your right to experience even your illusions. The same message can be found in the Bible:

> *Therefore God sends upon them a strong delusion,*
> *to make them believe what is false, so that all may*
> *be condemned who did not believe the truth but*
> *had pleasure in unrighteousness.*
>
> 2 Thess 2:11-12

The *Course* puts it this way:

> *I am responsible for what I see. I choose the*
> *feelings I experience, and decide upon the goal I*
> *would achieve. And everything that seems to*
> *happen to me I ask for, and receive as I have asked.*
>
> ACIM 21 II 2:3-5

The *Course* teaches that, although the world as understood by Man may be an Illusion, it can be experienced; it can also be believed to be a Real experience. A logical mind cannot accept this. That is precisely why so many cannot accept True Reality, and continue to use their intellectual minds to reinterpret the *Course*.

Many people in *Course* study groups have the same misunderstandings about the power or effects of their illusions. Not accepting erroneous beliefs can and does affect experience. Most people do not realize the beliefs they hold can cause them to remain lost within their own delusions forever.

One of the most common statements of students is, "In the end we are all going to get it." What they have failed to recognize is that Time is relevant to belief. As long as they are thinking in terms of Time, they are setting the stage for more experience within Time.

The *Course* speaks of Time as being both meaningful and unreal. Within the dream world of Ego, Time exists to provide experiences leading one to Truth (True Reality). Earlier in this book, you read that there are Dimensions within Creation. The *Course* speaks of them also, when referring to Time.

> *Miracles are part of an interlocking chain of forgiveness which, when completed, is the Atonement. Atonement works all the time in all the dimensions of time.*
>
> ACIM 1 I 25:1-2

> *The miracle is a learning device that lessens the need for time. It establishes an out-of pattern time interval not under the usual laws of time. In a sense it is timeless.*
>
> ACIM 1 I 47:1-3

This is not the first place where it has been stated that Time, as Man perceives it, is an Illusion.

> *People like us, who believe in physics, know that the distinction between past, present, and future is only a stubbornly persistent illusion.*

> Albert Einstein

Understanding the Illusion of Time is one of the most difficult stages in overcoming the delusions of this world. If you desire to experience True Reality, you must recognize that the concept of Time as viewed by Man will always stand in the way of his True Vision. Many here do not realize that Eternity is not going to begin. That which is Eternal is, was, and will always be *Now*.

From the *Course,* you find that Jesus was disclosing a new understanding, one that many miss even after years of study.

"No man cometh unto the Father but by me" does not mean that I am in any way separate or different from you except in time, and time does not really exist. The statement is more meaningful in terms of a vertical rather than a horizontal axis.

ACIM 1 II 4:1-2

In the horizontal reside the Dimensions of Time and space experienced within the illusory worlds of Judgment. In the vertical (non-judgment), True vision is experienced. This is why Jesus stated to mankind two thousand years ago not to judge anyone or any thing. All Judgment will cause you to see a distorted view of Reality.

The *Course* addresses this point and gives the reason for the continuous cycle Man is caught up in. It speaks of two complete thought systems, one based on Love (representing Reality), and the other based on Fear (representing that which is illusory or false). Whether one experiences the world from the awakened state of Atonement, or from its opposite (a world based upon the belief in Separation), one is subject to the laws of the world chosen. According to the *Course*, even the Illusionary world is not without power.

The *Course* focuses on training you to recognize and accept True Reality (Love) over Fear. It explains how no one can live any experience that did not originate with him or her. In this way, it teaches you to be responsible for the world you see.

Confusion is not uncommon when the human mind attempts to understand and then apply the laws from one system in another. According to the *Course*, this is impossible, because the two thought systems are different and opposite in every respect. The very idea of Time, for example, cannot be experienced the same way in the awakened and in the sleeping state.

In my Father's house are many rooms; *if it were
not so, would I have told you that I go to prepare a
place for you?*

Jn 14:2

Here Jesus was referring to Dimensions of Time, which are
part of the system that exists to be experienced. According to the
Course, although thoughts based on Fear and beliefs in Separation
are not Real, they are not without power or consequence. Each
thought will bring about an experience; the *Course* teaches that even
illusions are not without effects in terms of experience.

Without exception, each thought is subject to the laws of
Creation in either system. Within the world of Man, what you
project, you believe. What you believe, you will also perceive as
Real. This leads to a never-ending cycle of obscurity. Within the
thought system of the world of Man, what you call for, even your
illusions, must be honored.

If you are to experience Reality, *you* must be the one to
initiate the experience. You do this by exercising control over your
thoughts. The *Course*, like the Bible, clearly states that you have a
choice: to see things either as a human or as a Spirit. Not only are
you responsible for choosing one over the other, but you cannot
escape the consequences of the choice. Nor can you choose both
simultaneously.

As Jesus said, you cannot serve two masters. The *Course*
says that you must choose between Reality (Love) and Illusion
(Fear). It teaches that there is no gray area when it comes to Reality.

*One either sleeps or wakens. There is nothing in
between.*
ACIM: Workbook for Students, 140 2:5-6

To date, I have not encountered or heard of any teacher who
has totally accepted this simple precept! This has to be one of the

biggest challenges facing anyone who seeks a guru to interpret the *Course*.

Where does all this leave us? The *Course* summarizes itself as follows:

> *Nothing real can be threatened.*
> *Nothing unreal exists.*
> *Herein lies the peace of God.*

Distinguishing Reality from Illusion is the task faced by all of us in this world. The *Course* unequivocally states that this is the only (vitally important) job you have. Only what God Creates is Real; in fact, only God Creates. Man does not create—he *makes*. And what he makes is, by definition, unreal. Therefore, the man-made world is illusory.

"When we embrace the illusory we undergo the Death Experience."

In the *Course*, as in the Bible, you are presented with a Life or Death choice. Life represents Love, True Reality, and the True Self; Death represents Fear (the false self, the Ego, the human mind). Fear is something experienced. It is not Real. As in the Garden of Eden, where Adam and Eve chose to experience their own human minds as opposed to their Spiritual minds, when we embrace the illusory we undergo the Death Experience. Again, as Einstein put it, although the human mind and its product (the world) are an Illusion, they are "a persistent illusion."

Notwithstanding the illusion of this world, the vast majority of people continue to believe in it. Not only that, but they have misinterpreted many of the teachings of all the various prophets of God. Here of course I include the message of the Christ, which cannot be understood with a distorted or incomplete mind. The Bible states that the "wisdom" of this world is foolishness to God (1 Cor 3:19).

All or Nothing

The *Course* teaches that to honor either God, or the world, is to deny one or the other.

There is only one way out of the world's thinking, just as there was only one way into it. Understand totally by understanding totality.

ACIM 7 VII 10:9-10

Is "understanding totality" possible? One must first recognize the illusion (i.e., the dream state existing within the mind of Man). This is what Jesus was referring to when he spoke of overcoming this world:

He who has an ear, let him hear what the Spirit says to the churches. He who conquers shall not be hurt by the second death.

Rev 2:11

The world would have you believe that this is impossible. We are usually taught that we are and always will be sinners, incapable of Perfection. The Father has entrusted me with this message for you: Let go of this belief! And for all the religious teachers in this world, those who have kept the "Keys of the Kingdom" away from my children: Let my people go!

Two thousand years ago, Jesus declared that the time had come for an Awakening:

His disciples said to him, "When will the kingdom come?" "It will not come by watching for it. It will not be said, 'Look, here!' or 'Look, there!' Rather, the Father's kingdom is spread out upon the earth, and people don't see it."

Thom 113

Just as it was time then, it is time *now*. It will always be the right time to accept Love (God) over your human agenda and erroneous beliefs.

In the *Course*, Jesus said this about Time:

> *Delay does not matter in eternity, but it is tragic in time. You have elected to be in time rather than eternity, and therefore believe you are in time. Yet your election is both free and alterable. You do not belong in time. Your place is only in eternity, where God Himself placed you forever.*

ACIM 5 VI 1:3-7

> *Your resurrection is your reawakening. I am the model for rebirth, but rebirth itself is merely the dawning on your mind of what is already in it.*

ACIM 6 I 7:1-2

Whether you accept it or not, what you believe will affect your experience.

> *You may believe you are responsible for what you do, but not for what you think. The truth is that you are responsible for what you think, because it is at this level that you can exercise choice. What you do comes from what you think. You cannot separate yourself from the truth by "giving" autonomy to behavior.*

ACIM 2 VI 2:5-8

To sum up: in order to see Reality, you must use a new set of eyes. For that which you seek already exists, and you do not see it yet. The *Course* was written to develop these eyes, by training your mind to reinterpret this world and everything in it. It does this in a gradual way, by teaching forgiveness. First, it teaches you to forgive others by realizing that you are not in a position to be their judge; then it leads you to understand that, in terms of Reality, forgiveness is not necessary.

In Reality there is nothing but Perfect Love.

That which you seek already exists

The Ultimate Choice!

In closing, I would like to thank you for reading this book. When I was instructed by the Father to deliver this message, at first I had to deal with my own fears. They seemed overwhelming, but as I allowed the release of my Ego-based mind, Spirit filled me with an understanding that is available to all.

In the Gospel of Thomas, Jesus stated that the best way to understand was to understand the beginning:

> *The disciples said to Jesus: Tell us how our end
> will be. Jesus said: Since you have discovered the*

beginning, why do you seek the end? For where the beginning is, there will the end be. Blessed is he who shall stand at the beginning (in the beginning), and he shall know the end, and shall not taste death.

Thom 18

Each one of us is faced with the same choice: to hold on to Judgment or to release it. One decision brings you salvation, and the other brings you damnation. For the sake of all...please choose Love.

For all those who have ears to hear and eyes to see and the willingness to commit their whole being to do the will of our Father, I say:

Welcome Home!

Glossary

Atonement Consciousness
Same as the Christ Consciousness—being aware of Unconditional Love and God as One. The perfected state is Perfect Love.

Christ Consciousness
The state of Awareness that is fully awakened to Perfect Love; being beyond all Judgment.

Collective Consciousness
The sum of Energy produced by the Genuine Will of all persons present in this world.

Consciousness
That which pertains to Awareness, both in the human sense and in the spiritual.

Dimension
A Plane of Creation operating within a particular frequency range of energy.

Duality
A system based on opposites: positive and negative, good and bad, awake and asleep, Life and Death, etc.

Ego
The Lower Self: that part of Soul that identifies with the physical personality self of this world.

Eternal Moment
Another way of saying Eternity, which comprises past, present, and future occurring simultaneously outside of the confines of linear motion. The ever present *Now*.

Evolution
Progression and development of something in a linear or unfolding manner.

False Essence
That part of Soul that identifies with this world, holding that the physical is True Reality. The Ego, the False self.

Fate
That which is set to occur in the future within the world of time, based upon a continuation of a specific energy flow on an undisturbed path.

Form
The appearance of something relative to the senses.

Frequency
The rate at which all energy, including thought, vibrates.

Genuine Will
That which is truly believed, as opposed to stated belief.

God
That Which Is. The summation of everything

God the Father/Mother
The Creator, absolute Pure Consciousness; the summation of All That Is, both seen and unseen.

God the Holy Spirit
The unit of Consciousness, begotten of the Creator for the sole purpose of allowing for the experience of degrees or levels of Awareness. The bridge between the Real and the Imagined; the orchestrator of the interplay between all Dimensions within Creation.

God the Son
An individualized aspect of the Creator's Consciousness. He who was begotten of the Father/Mother.

Higher Self
That part of Soul that identifies with the Spiritual realms.

I Am
That part of Soul that resides at its core. The ultimate determiner of experience; the real decision-maker beyond the Ego.

Judgment
Evaluating something based on a system of Duality, i.e. Good versus Evil. That which precludes an outcome.

Karma
The law of Balance. The impersonal system of energy that restores equilibrium to the unbalanced.

Matrix of Creation
The interconnected system established for experience. It is composed of various Dimensions, both seen and unseen. "In My Father's House there are many mansions."

Movement
A change or shift in terms of energy, either in this world or in the worlds beyond.

Observation
Witnessing something with no determination as to whether it is positive or negative.

Separation
A perceived experience, based on the belief that something can exist outside of All That Is (God).

Sonship
The second person of the Trinity. The term refers to the collective group of Souls (individualized units of Consciousness).

Soul
That which was begotten of the Creator. The sum total of the I Am, the Ego, and the Higher Self.

Time
A measured interval in which something is experienced, i.e. a moment, an hour, a year, an eon...

True Essence
That part of Soul which is Real. That which exists beyond the illusory world; the Higher Self or the True Self.

True, or Ultimate, Reality
That which exists beyond the veil of Illusion.

Truth
That which is beyond perception.

Veil
The image, existing within a judgmental mind, that clouds True Reality.

Vibration
Rate of frequency of energy, including thought.

World
The term used by Man to identify both this planet and this Dimension.

Index

Entries in bold denote Glossary items; page numbers in italics denote diagrams

Index of Scriptural References